Dedicated to my friends at the University of Essex. For without them I wouldn't be the rebel as I am now. I am the Autistic Conservative. And to my friend Hannah, for getting me take up writing again.

Introduction

I wrote a novella that was originally released in February 2007. This novella was bizarrely titled with an elongated tongue twisting name called 'A Baffling Unoriginal Looking with Voice to Prove Positive'. Why that long title, because as an autistic author and as it's a story about autism I felt that it would work to make it fit in with other books about autism at the time. A few years before 'A Baffling Unoriginal' was released there was another book about an autistic detective called 'The Curious Incident of the Dog in the Night Time'. It was quite a big success and I thought that kind of name made people think that it was about an unconventional hero with some interesting features. That gave me the idea that giving my own novella an unusual name would help to sell it as a story about autism.

A Puzzle in a Tunnel's novella is a philosophical fictional work. It was inspired by the stories of political ideologies written in novel form by the classic writers of Orwell, Dickens, Rand, Twain and Huxley. Back in the day before films and TV shows dramatized the politics of fictional societies these writers wrote their philosophies and their settings as fictional works that illustrates and captures the potential of different ways of living. Such as Atlas Shrugged being a novel about objectivism or Nineteen Eighty-Four being about totalitarianism. I wanted to reinvent this classic genre for a contemporary setting that could capture the public's imagination. But in this age of the world-wide web, such a book would not be taken in the same way. So now for this new edition I have created a part fiction, part non-fiction book to show how my ideas of society can work with a fiction piece to dramatize the ideas in a craft like that of Douglas Adam's Hitchhikers Guide to the Galaxy.

This novella was based on a story that I wrote for a creative writing course at an evening school. The story was quite good and my tutor said that I had all the makings of a novelist. The story behind 'A Baffling Unoriginal' was partly based on my life. At that point in time I was a frustrated and isolated person struggling to be accepted. I have Aspergers syndrome, a mild form of autism that affects my ability to interact with people with communication and relationship difficulties. And to be consumed with obsessive interests in a limited variety of subjects. During my childhood and right up to when I was in my late teens I had never been interested in learning about my disability because I was in denial about my condition, especially because of the stigma associated with having a disability back then. I refused to accept my diagnoses at the time because to me it was like a death sentence that ostracised me from the community. To make matters worse although I had some disability support workers I never got any formal disability management programme or social skills training. I had to practice self-care and learn about interacting with people by the time I was grown up.

When I was practicing self-care I started to become more independent of my peers. I didn't want to be the stereotypical disabled person that relies on carers and living out of social welfare benefits. I wanted to be somebody of distinction and significance, but it was a struggle to be accepted. I grew up at a time when New Labour with it's social liberal ideas was creating ways to embrace diversity. Although these ideas were good, not all those ideas were for the better. In my case as a disabled person I was being accepted not by my abilities, but by the limitations of my impairments as if I was supposed to accept a lifetime of welfare and accept the care system of the state instead of finding a way to advance my desire to better myself. That for me was like being forced into slavery. Such an attitude like that drove me to be a Conservative and right wing radical autistic. Which is what is explored in this book.

The book has now become a novella intertwined with some sections that I have written about how I have lived with my autism, the politics and social issues of autism and other disabilities and my ideas on how the best qualities of being autistic can benefit the world. I felt that I had to release this book once again with a different structure, but rewritten in a way that suits the need to justify the case for accepting autism in an active and positive way. The reason for this is because in recent years I have become politically active in my abilities and I have found some useful allies in politics, sport and the arts. I am now an archer with a campaign to promote the further inclusion of minority sports, I read and write about ideas for politics and science, I have spent the last ten years studying science as a distance learning student and practicing my skills as a hobbyist. I may have been unemployed and on welfare but I haven't been idle. I keep trying to better myself because I refuse to give into defeat. Walt Disney was fired from a newspaper because he 'lacked imagination and had no original ideas'. Years later when he built his entertainment empire Disney Inc. bought out that very newspaper that fired him in a sweet vengeance from beyond the grave. Having heard that story I decided to go back to creative writing. My mind is full of ideas and creative suggestions that I had to get back into it.

You might find some of the style of the writing of 'A Baffling Unoriginal' to be as bizarre as the title and that was what my intention was at the time. The reason for this is because at that point in time I was reading and writing in a monotropic way. This is a way to describe an autistic person's social and cognitive functions in which they have limited interests and they can only pay attention to what's in their own attention tunnel. In which case I had an ability to communicate with certain words that I could rephrase from what I already knew. I hadn't had a proper social skill set growing up and in effect I frequently repeated certain words in a peculiar way. That explains the use of language. One critic who did an appraisal of my book likened my style to that of James Joyce's 'Ulysses'. I later checked the differences between Ulysses and A Baffling Unoriginal and it was very similar. I think that is perhaps the best compliment I have ever had for my work.

One thing that should be noted about this story is that it is not the first edition. This is a case where the novella has been drastically rewritten and that can make this novella sound like a whole new book. As it turns out a writer can self-plagiarise his work where the original story didn't add up to make the story work right. It might sound like as if this is a completely different novel, but it isn't because the original manuscript has been rewritten by myself. I found it hard to begin with but as I looked back at the use of words and grammar in the first edition I realised just how far I had come since I first entered the publishing world. At that time I hadn't been able to properly express myself but through my writing I practiced using a technique which involved streaming my conscious into the writing which flowed from my imagination into the text. With this I created something that looked like a scripture that resembled all the terrible injustice that I was seeing through my eyes and I was the rebel that wanted to unleash my bright soul into this wild world. Ten years on I found that my use of words had improved in my writing and was able to express myself better. This made me realise that in the first edition I hadn't really proved a positive point about autism, instead I was just channelling my mental energy from my distaste about the world into a story that was implausible for some people to understand. To that end I decided to rewrite the story and make it focus on a point to prove positive about autism.

I don't count the novella itself as my biggest achievement even though it was my first published novella. A few months after the book was released I checked to see if there were any other autistic authors out there. I discovered that at 21, I hold the world record as the world's youngest published autistic novelist.

Although I have had some very bad life's experiences growing up I never let those things keep me back. I think it may be attributed to my stubbornness to give into the limitations of my disability as my teachers and study support workers had done. All forms of life were created unequal in nature and we should accept all classes of citizens into society. I don't want sympathy, I want acceptance.

CHAPTER ONE

Desperate for an inspiration Scott Hardy left the job centre. He had been up late wondering what made the future so discerning for him. It wasn't easy for him as he had an autistic spectrum disorder. He had just presented a rejection letter to the customer staff at the employment services. Hoping it was possible for a job in the news industry his employment consultant could only tell him once again that he was under qualified. It had become very predictable. For the most part his place on the autistic spectrum made him very knowledgeable in many areas, he didn't care if it made him under qualified in anyway. If it were possible to demonstrate to people that autism had provided him with some advantage, then perhaps he could prove them wrong.

Scott actually did have a job working in the press, but it wasn't a full-time profession. He had been doing a few articles for a newspaper called Beyond London as a freelance journalist. He only does work for them on a basis of providing subliminal features and reviews. He wasn't really made for the stuff of a straight write up job.

On the way home he decided to walk so as to avoid paying for a bus fare. He had been quite used to this routine as he had done it several times before. He was somewhat obsessively compulsive in his management of money and in particular with the contents of his bank account. Worried that he might end up in such a debt that he watched it constantly every week to make sure that he didn't go broke.

Therefore he set a target of keeping the amount of his account to be no lower than £1000. He may seem like a tightwad but at least it helps. *Greatest autistic advantage: Give in to compulsory measures. Watch what you use and preserve whatever you can. You never know when a big bill may come along.*

All in all he was demoralised with frustration by the ways there was hardly a place for him every fortnight coming home from that Jobcentre. He didn't even have much desire to interact with people or get out much so you wouldn't really catch a person like him going into a life of crime or turbulence. He was desperate to prove a point and he did not want to be stuck in a catch-22 situation for his whole life. 'The problem with these people is that they can't see any usefulness in me.' He said to himself. Scott was frustrated even more with his ability to express himself to people. Sometimes he said things without intentionally meaning them and it made him feel stupid and embarrassed with himself. *It's not my fault I ended up the way I am. I was made to think of myself that way.*

He would use the advantages of his disability to make something useful for himself. To fit his obsession with everything looking brand new he would clean up the house so that it didn't look like it was getting old. He hated getting old, at 22 he felt like he hadn't gone anywhere. Most people his age had made it into a career and probably got on the housing market. But Scott was stuck at home made to feel like he was hopeless. It was not a good situation to be in with his autism. Once there was a time when he threatened to kill himself because his life was not going the way he wanted, but he was too stubborn to give into defeat. To cope with his sense of despair he took up shadowboxing to control his stress levels and give him a stable mental edge. He chose to box at invisible forces because they represented the negative thoughts in his head that looked like a complacent being that made him feel like a slave bound by his impairment.

CHAPTER TWO

Scott got onto his computer feeling absolutely dull. Just as he flicked the switch he quickly set up the browser. His mother was at work until the afternoon and there was no one else in the house. Scott was the one who occupied the house most of the time. Dividing himself between looking for work and trying to self-employ through his part time journalism work. Sometimes he wanted to move out and find something to fill the solitude. So instead he preferred to stay indoors for pretty much most of the time unless he felt like he had to leave for some reason.

He logged onto the web just going through a few fan websites before signing into his email. When he got there he found only a few bits of the odd junk mail. One was a discount sale at Play.com and the other being a reply to a question he sent to the BBC for guidelines in the script department. There was no reply from the editor of Beyond London.

After doing a bit of research for work and writing, he broke for lunch. But for some reason he didn't feel like eating as he was sick to the stomach. He had been taking the time to evaluate and see where his futile position had come and gone. He only had one article published so far and it had been three months since his last writing job.

A little earlier than usual his mother June had come in. She heard Scott making an unusual gesture to himself involving speaking at total nothingness until she butted in. 'Who are you talking to?' she asked.

Scott stood to attention in a manner like he'd just escaped a form of hypnosis.

'I was just enjoying some quiet thinking time.' said Scott. His mode of speech was lacking in prosody. This meant that he couldn't pronounce his sentences with the same feeling. Lashing out without sounding angry or proclaiming his innocence in a mild tone.

'Well it sounded like you were talking to yourself.' said June. 'You know what I keep telling you about doing that.'

'It's just my way of exercising my imagination, mum.' Scott twittered his arms and hands about in a kind of sloppy motion. This act of motor clumsiness was very common to his condition that many people have misinterpreted it as rudeness. 'It's how I like to think and be myself.'

'Oh don't be silly.'

'Well what's wrong with that.' said Scott. 'I don't necessarily care as I'd rather be free to use...whatever I want to do with myself.'

'But it's still making you look stupid. You look more like you're hypnotised or something.' Said June. 'You're just being neurotic.'

'No I'm not!'

June had something else to get off her chest for a moment that she didn't say anything else. She had stopped talking about her feelings to Scott from a younger age of his life. He would take them as a literal interpretation. When he was younger he wasn't all that familiar with idioms and phrases. The older he grew over time he started to realise what all these things meant and starting using them. Things like 'Has the cat got your tongue', Out of the blue' and

'Pull yourself together' were always a laugh when he couldn't understand them. There was this one time that he mentioned an idiom that made everyone laugh at him. No one bothered to correct him and he just flipped out at the way his words made him look stupid. He was so angry he almost walked out. It got a member of staff to intervene who almost felt like slapping him, but luckily he managed to explain himself in a flash.

'How did it go down the jobcentre then?' asked June.

'Not too good I'm afraid.' he said. 'I would rather take up my own self-made job as a career.'

'But you can't, not when you haven't got any income from it.'

'Yes I know that.' said Scott with unprojected agony. 'I can now understand what you and your side of the family have in common.'

'What?'

'Well you all have a sense of cowardice that you don't even admit to.' stated Scott. 'If the old girl next door got burgled and you know it you'd wait till he's gone.'

'Shut up.' June knew what he meant. He was still angry at the lack of action that his mother took on his problems. It was so distressing for her to watch this little boy of hers get angry at the things that upset him personally. But even when she tried to explain to him he was not emphatic enough to understand.

'You don't think I know how to stand up and make a decision for myself.' Said Scott.

'That's not the point.' Said June.

'Well I can when I want to, you sick trouble shooter.' Scott retorted barely loud. At least a social worker could understand as June couldn't. 'At least I know how to make a living for myself better than you do...you wretched failure.' June was shocked and horrified at this. Maybe there was more to Scott that she hadn't realised. June's lack of attention to his mental issues wasn't because of neglect but because she felt distraught at the knowledge of her son's mental health. Scott was desperate to learn quickly about his autism for fear that he would be unable to fit in with society. What made him resent his autism wasn't his mental issues, but the way that he was belittled and stigmatised. He wanted to show the benefits of his disability that could help others.

'Oi! What was that last remark about me being a failure.' she demanded.

'Maybe I'm disabled but I'm not some stereotypical infidel. Disabilities have a beautiful side to them in ousting problem people like you.' Scott didn't need special needs right now. All he knew he could count on were his guts.

'I've done a lot for you. I brought you up and I've cared for you.' June took the look of her son as a misstatement because he only took his own side.

'Maybe, but you can't disarm me with sympathy stories.' Whenever he was interacting with his peers Scott was always the same. Trusting his own side so much that he only took it from his point of view.

'You should know better I'm your mother. I thought you had a good deal of moral sense unlike all the other kids you went to school with. What was it you told me: Would be bastards who haven't got any purpose in life. Lazy and good for nothing.'

'Maybe, but I 'am suffering under my own terms.'

'What kind of terms?'

It took Scott a while to put the information together. His mind barely grasped information that it hadn't used before. But at the same time he could jog someone's memory by withering on a different subject. 'Well what about my time in education. Okay so maybe I got off with a few qualifications. But that places you sent me to very nearly cost me my life. It was a stupid community school, the kind made for kids who are supposedly born stupid. Years of rote learning and no challenging stuff. It was so boring I once threw an entire stock load of books out of the library window.' Scott didn't care for his out of sync tone as long as he could make enough sense.

'I remember that, you threaten to kill yourself and scarred me for days.' June barely remembered the dark trauma. It was like Scott was punishing her for making him suffer with his disability. She couldn't get a wink of sleep for a week that both of them were recommended by the school to get in talks with a social worker.

'Well maybe if I knew my life would end up like this then I should have taken my belt and used it for a noose. None of those special needs teachers were any good. They insisted on schoolwork only, no bother about your mental issues. Political correctness was making them useless and therefore I had to leave school a year early. I bet you waiting for me to cry wolf or cry out or cry water weren't you? Hey!'

'Stop it!' insisted June. 'It's not making any difference.' It really hurt her so much that June almost expected the conclusion that she was a bad mother.

'What about the two years at college studying journalism.' Scott went on. 'I thought I could've done better there. Instead of which I ended up in a futile youth hostel. I was so close to getting involved in that blade fight in the refectory. Some rubber faced bastard come up to me calling me a gay just because I was autistic. Homophobes accuse gays of perverted and therefore mentally ill and since I had a mental health issue he thought he was gay. He even wanted to unleash my instability because I could make a useful dog to have a fight with.'

'A what?'

'A dog! Can't you listen to me well enough?'

'Well I'm sorry son, but considering how you struggle to speak to me I can't get through to you.'

Scott sighed and breathed into his palms to try and calm his senses.

June thought she'd ran away from all this. Since they'd left West London all those years ago June thought she had escaped the bad upbringing that influenced his thinking and had a very bad effect on his autistic spectrum disorder. The anxiety and frustrated that burned within him made him feel a degree of intelligence and acute self-awareness. In Scott's case he was always vaguely aware using the clear signs of his disability. Taking the advantage of his autism was something he pursued with utmost integrity. Scott had hardly got anywhere since leaving college and was desperate to make his mark on the world. But he wasn't wanted no matter what he tried to do.

'Why can't you just go forward and not look back?' insisted June.

'Well because those mistakes in the past have not even left me yet.' said Scott. 'That's why! Haven't you ever considered how the effect of my past has disabled my future? Don't you realise that my lack of mental awareness tutoring made me stupid and incompetent. And the people who I like to interact with have avoided me and given me the cold shoulder because my inability to form friendships with them has led to me being unable to build connections with them. How do expect me to get on with life when my mental issues make it close to impossible for me to express myself?'

'There is nothing that no one can do about it Scott.' said June, given in as if she's won the fight.

'Liar!' Scott got to his feet. Fed up regarded as a mentally retarded person with absolutely no prospects enshrouded in fantasy ethics. 'You know what you can make for yourself if you try. Make a stand and say no right in the face of them. Instead of pretending to be an ordinary citizen and think you can get over it, you stupid old bag. You're just too old to raise me now.'

'That was not the idea.' said June. She turned to storm off upstairs. Scott could only sit there as he just couldn't understand any human. He had got fed up with her way, as it was only shooting trouble at him.

Scott went up to his bedroom. The time was right to make a very big decision. Right now he needed to be somebody for his own good. He packed a bag full of clothes along with a notebook, his micro cassette recorder, his digital camera and a newspaper. A positive solution to his problems might just be along the way. He took out a half written piece of paper from his note book and tore off the blank half. He always made sure he didn't use just one scrap of paper just for a list or a reminder. He wrote: Dear Mum, I need some spare time on my own right now. I will be heading to Auntie Jackie's place in Islington.

Scott took his keys and credit card forgetting spare change and headed for the door. Leaving the note on his way out.

CHAPTER THREE

Scott thought for a long time about how he reconsidered his family values. He wasn't really a big fan of snap decisions. 22 years old and yet he's barely changed himself. Scott had always been very anxious of his motives, as life was a social minefield for him capable of putting a foot wrong. Whatever he encountered in this battlefield he didn't let it and or anyone hold him back.

Looking for the right place to find solitude Scott took the train at Canada Water tube station. A route he was very used to from this station. On his way all he could do was give into what was running through his mind. Thinking of trains and the pattern of his route through the Underground. Playing with his imagination was his favourite autistic behavioural pattern. However when it comes to work it all becomes too much of an obsession. Typing up a memo and thinking in free time is always a struggling session.

As Scott got off the East London line at Whitechapel he changed to the Hammersmith and City line. *As always maps are so bloody easy for me.* He looked up at the notices for directions. As he walked up the stairs to the next platform he saw very few station staff on duty. It's a lot different from his home in Canary Wharf where the commuters have got the most slap up gear on hand at their disposal. *Why can't every station be as secure as it is in the business sector?*

Scott's knowledge of the railways was from a childhood hobby. He used to obsessively read about trains and collected toy models of his favourite locomotives. The thing drew him to this obsession was the stylistic patterns of the way tracks were designed that represented his pattern thinking abilities. This is just one of three sets of thinking patterns that autistic people have. And he also enjoyed the colourful stylish designs of the trains themselves that had a distinct character that almost looked like it was a personalised journey to the places that he liked to travel. His knowledge of trains covered the mechanical workings, the journeys they travelled and the lines they ran on, and the companies that owned them. It was this passion for travel and his love of the railways that were combined to make him become a travel writer. But he wasn't an active train traveller for most of the time, because of the cost of the journeys themselves.

The yearly rises in train and bus fares bothered him the most. That's why he was he preferred to be tight. He had enough fortitude to complain unlike most people advised to cope. *Bloody Mayor! Topping up fares to fill up his wallet. Thickie Bastard, as is the rest of the council.*

When he reached Moorgate Scott made another transaction onto the Northern Line. This time he wasn't thinking except for the sights around him. By the time he reached Moorgate station Scott had exercised his imagination so much that he almost lost his way. From Moorgate onwards only another five stations to go, bearing in mind the tube map revealed the actual distances between the stations. If only the trains could move like a passing thought, then Scott wouldn't be listening to the floundering activity in his brain. *I'm not going to think about that woman. I might have been negative, but I was thinking with a lot more common sense than she can care to admit.*

Finally, when Scott got out of Camden Town station he made his way up to go to his Grandparent's place in Buck Street. He was terribly cautious by the awful sight of the council houses. Just capping his eyes on it was enough to make him feel slaughtered. *Why here? What kind of people could live like this in battery pens? It's like the aftermath of the Towering Inferno compared to the Docklands.*

On the ground floor of the flat lived Scott's grandparents. The route from his South London house to this North London flat had been taken several times beforehand. Scott's uncle was a market dealer who would drop off cut price fruit and veg to his house. Scott wasn't exactly fond of greens as his taste buds were hyper allergic. When he was younger he would take his grandparent's share of the food to them on chores. But when Scott stopped making visits to avoid expensive tickets his uncle started to take over the deliveries.

Just as he was about to open the door, he found a scene between a couple on the outside road to the flat. 'Business as usual round 'ere' was the expression for this. Changing the ways of these god forsaken crime ridden estates would be one of the many things that Scott would like to resolve. Modernising for the families that live around here, making better community centres for people to work together, encourage youths to open up business around here. Get them away from crime in all the better of ways instead of watching them take out their frustration on the residents for kicks. *Bloody troublemakers, always taking it out on ordinary folk like their surrounded by punch bags.*

Scott just admired the sight as the row dissipated. Now as a journalist it would be expected for him to take note of the situation for a newspaper. But Scott hated it. *That's not news, it's propaganda for gang warfare. Maybe everyone has a right to know, but human rights have no right to force the publication of fascist movements.* He stopped thinking aloud when he opened the door. 'Hello?' he said.

'I'm in here sweetheart.' called and old lady voice. Scott recognised it as his auntie Jackie. 'Your mum said that you'd be coming.' There again Jackie realised her niece had trouble with life's problems. *Well at least Mum knows guesses about my whereabouts.*

Scott went into the living room to find her with the radio playing in the background listening to the commentator on Radio 4. He stood there casually trying to think of the situation. He was still determined not to have his disability used against him and was aware of the enormity of the anger if he went too far.

'Before you say anything I just want to make it clear that I'm not making up with that stupid old bag.' said Scott. 'Maybe she's right to have brought me up, but from my point of view that's all I'm taking.'

Jackie slapped Scott in anger. He submitted to this course of satisfaction, as to feel just how much he had gone to get out. He didn't react well because to him a slap was something his senses had conquered. The impact of a fist was a driving point to lash out.

'You watch your bloody language 'round ere.' Jackie retorted. 'You might be disabled but that's not an excuse to slag your mother off!'

'Your right, I'm sorry I've...I...' Scott tried to explain his side. Each side of his mind was telling him what's wrong or right. Which was the most important: his strong vantages for him or being guiltily oppressive towards his peers? '...oh I don't know! I'm just lost!' Like a battle wary fighter he slumped down into the armchair holding his hands above his head. This was usually a mark of surrender but Scott signified it for a position of social exile.

'Alright then, what have you got to moan about this time?' At least Jackie had some sympathy for him.

'It couldn't be a moan.' humoured Scott. 'How did I end up like this?' Not even afraid to confess he went on. 'I 'am just totally downtrodden. Here I' am trying to make something of myself and yet all that comes out of it is utter unfairness. I'M NOTHING BUT A COMPLETE HIDEOUS JOKE!' He took a deep sigh. 'You know what...maybe I should've swung when I had the chance. I'm not getting anything out of life due to problematic trouble shooters.'

'Your just like that manic depressive who lives upstairs from us.' said Jackie. 'Well used to live upstairs. He copped it after his last psychiatric appointment. Looked back on his life and thought he was useless.' 'You mean he's dead?' asked Scott.

'Correct.' said Jackie. 'It's a pity you're not mad like him. Otherwise you would have done it years ago. I mean really what else could you ask for?'

'You wouldn't understand...and I don't think anyone in the world either would or could. Do you think its easy living with autism? Sometimes I think you forget what this thing gives me that either holds me back or pushes me forward.' Scott's odd dialogue was described as idiosyncratic. A lingual type of self-made grammar speaking in the way he drew information from his brain in the form of what he saw from his point of view.

'You think and talk in pictures.' said Jackie. 'It's not my fault I can't understand.' Scott shuddered as he motioned in an odd posture. Almost like he was going to be sick. 'Well what else can I do? I don't know much about what to do with you?'

'Maybe if I didn't have too few friends then I wouldn't be in this crisis.' Scott slumped backwards into the armchair. 'No. Perhaps I just don't need them. Maybe my ambitions worked better if I spent most of my time as an exile from society wondering about the realities of life.'

'Look you should forget about other people.' Jackie pointed out. 'You should be thinking about yourself. Never mind the way they think of you with your disability; never mind your bloody pathetic school and never mind about senseless backbiting at home. You've got to go about with life your own way.'

'Don't you think I know that? Because this is just about as much as I can make of myself Auntie.

Nobody wants an autistic person as an employee. God help it that bloody jobcentre is hardly any help. What's the point of it if it can't help me find work?'

'Don't you worry about that. You've got your whole life ahead of you.'

'I know you keep saying.' said Scott. 'But how much of my life is left ahead of me? This is making my patience tick!' Coping with anything was always part of Scott's job. Incompetence was the biggest thing he needed to tackle. In the years since he left college he had absolutely no access to a workplace to get some income. 'I want to be something now! If only that stupid woman gave me a better opportunity.'

'Well then do it now.' she shrugged. 'There is a better place out there that needs someone like you.'

'But where...where is it? I know the advantages this can give me.' he stroked the sides of his brain. 'How the hell can I prove them when I'm invisibly labelled as a weakling?' He thought about the memories Jackie's late neighbour brought to him. After he finished his education Scott tried to deliberately kill himself. His prospects were just as nil as they were now. *Maybe it would have been better off I had the courage to get out of this world. Of all those attempts to blend in with society, none of them worked out. I just haven't got a place to mark myself!*

CHAPTER FOUR

Scott wreaked with angst as his mobile alarm went off at six in the morning. He looked at the date on the LCD: Thurs 13th April 2006. *The end of the working week. Or how I can't get the hang of Thursdays.* Totally exhausted from a panicking night sweat he quickly got out of bed. Scott was a very mysterious person, but he didn't get much liaising. He thought about the positive aspects of life to cope with it. When he considered suicide it he was put off by his stubbornness to give in and through self-help and learning to love life.

First thing in the kitchen was boiling the kettle. He got a cup out of the cupboard and then got the milk from the fridge. Although he didn't touch a drop last night he felt like he had a hangover. The heated exchange was bad for his super sensitivity. Making him anxiously traumatic. Collocating with self-made work Scott started toasting some bread for breakfast.

Just then the phone ran and Scott went to pick it up. It was a message from a man he knew from one of his favourite TV programmes. An avid obsessive of Doctor Who and Great Railway Adventures, Scott worked it out in a heartbeat...it was Tom Baker! 'Bloody hell!'

As soon as the message finished he put the phone down. Next he tapped in his home number. Before tapping half the number he stopped to reconsider. *Ohh, what the hell. At least I can just see if she's fine for Auntie.* So he pressed June written on the second autodial button and picked up the receiver. 'Hello.' he said. 'Mum are you there.'

'What.' there was surprising tone on the other end. Scott only assumed that she misheard him. But he realised that she was after what he had to say, having drawn from previous experience.

'I just got a phone call from the fourth Doctor, alias Tom Baker.' he said.

'I know.' she laughed.

'You wot!' he said. 'Oh yeah, I know what you're talking about. That new voice message thing that he's doing for BT.'

'Yes that's correct. So when are you coming home?'

'Maybe sometime later.' said Scott. 'Look I didn't mean to walk out like that just because I got fed up. I just thought you had lost the understanding that I was autistic. It's like as if you had forgotten who I was for a while.'

'Don't be such a baby Scott. I only wanted what was best for you that was all.'

'And look what it got me.' Scott pointed out. 'Answer me this: did you ever, ever, ever look at what you were getting me into?'

June was speechless. 'I'm sorry Scott, I just couldn't think of what to do with you. When you're in school I had to make your education choices for you.'

'Well then maybe I should have made that decision for myself all those years ago.' he blasted without the right tone. 'Maybe I didn't know what to do, but at least you did something about it. More's the pity it didn't work.' They both took a moment. But as actions were more than words, healing couldn't be done over the phone. 'Look maybe it would be better if we talked about this at home. Okay.'

'Well alright then.' said June. 'It's not that I feel all the flabbergasted. I just...struggle to understand you, but I just can't stand your way of making decisions.'

'Well that's not my problem.' said Scott. 'You see Mum, it works like this. I struggle to express myself to people so when I am angry I can only say in a certain way. It is through a use of words that only a few people can understand. That's why my mode of speech is a bit difficult to follow. I would like to improve it but I just don't have anything at my disposal. I know I lack empathy, but I don't want sympathy, I want respect. See ya later. Thanks for arranging that thing with Tom by the way.' Scott put the phone down. *Maybe I shouldn't have come here in the first place. Maybe I should've tried spending my money on my own accommodation.*

A while later Scott's mobile rang for a call that he had long been waiting for. 'Hello Scott, its Georgia from Beyond London here.' It was the newspaper that gave Scott his first publication. However it was in need of more than what Scott had already given them.

'Hello Georgia, what's up.'

'Listen Scott, I've had a bit of time to consider your latest proposal and perhaps I can give you a little job to do.'

'Fabulous.'

'I've also tried to get through to you at home.' she said.

'Ah...well I suppose you now know that I've been through a rough patch recently.' said Scott. His weak tone was not really anything embarrassing or emotional.

'Well that's life!' she didn't take his feelings seriously enough. Her life was always automatically info taking. Encouraging her workmates to be pushy when they needed to be.

'But still never mind about all that. You know I don't like family values.' Scott hardly sounded like he'd regretted it. 'What did you have to say about my latest proposal then?'

Scott had made a proposal to Georgia to try and show how ambitious he was. He wasn't going to let his autism constrain him or have other people make things easy for him with low expectations of awkwardness. Having enough of writing for small features he was determined to do a big review of a museum far away from where he would normally be assigned. *Enough of the London centric reports, I want to get out beyond London. Now there's the real deal.* So Scott thought of an idea to explore the trains that he had read about in his childhood books from encyclopaedias he indulged in like scrumptious confectionary. One of his dream holidays was taking a trip to York to see the classic locomotives on display at the National Railway Museum. He had seen enough travel leaflets to fill his house and was now determined to go there once and for all. The idea was to write a piece on the features of the museum focusing on the museum's roundhouse where all the trains where kept.

'I like the idea and I've decided to give you a commission after all. However I can't give you the job because of at this time I can't cover travel expenses for you.'

'What!' exclaimed Scott. 'I thought you liked it.'

'I do but at this time I haven't got any money to spare for a travel expenses.' Said Georgia. 'But I have got something else that you might like.'

'Okay then, I'm not too disheartened.' Said Scott keeping his cool. 'What is it?'

'One of my contacts at Time Out needs a review of a newly refurbished expo at the London Transport Museum. Would you be willing to take it? I know it's not what you had in mind but I think it might be a good idea to try someplace else.'

'Well that's okay then.' Said Scott enthusiastically. 'I'll take it.'

'Great, I knew you'd be okay with it.' Said Georgia. 'Now I will give you the brief, have you got a pen and paper? It will have to be - '

'Hang on a moment.' Scott made for a notebook on the table. 'Let me take this down. Right go on.'

'It's 250 to 300 words in length.' Said Georgia.

'Right!'

'Have you got a camera?'

'Yes indeedy.' He was prancing about like an ecstatic four-year-old. 'I might have to ask the staff about that one, because most of the major exhibitions that I've been to in the past have barred cameras from all the special exhibitions.'

'Well then you'll have to get in touch with the press office. Ask them if they can get anything if you can't take pictures.' Said Georgia.

'Okay, don't worry about opening times and websites because I've got that already.' Said Scott.

'Right, well it's got to be in by July 18, which is when we're going to press.'

'Very well, oh and thank you for the commission.' to which he quickly hung up. 'FANTASTIC!'

CHAPTER FIVE

From the moment he got the call Scott was anxiously motivated to get on with it. Wasting no time he rushed to get washed and dressed. He got his coat to pocket his hand held tape recorder, notebook and digital camera. So excited he almost forgot the time, as it was the trains were currently selling peak tickets. *Oh what the hell, there's a big pile of cash coming from the editor when this is in print.* Unbothered to wake Jackie up, he wrote on the pad near the phone: Dear Auntie, I have just got a writing job from Beyond London. I will be out for most of the day and I won't be coming back here. Scott.

The note had made him remember his mobile, so he went back to his makeshift bed to get it before going out. It had also come to his attention that his trip to the North of England would require an overnight bag. Having travelled to Jackie's house several times before he knew he'd have a supply of fresh clothes there from previous stay overs so he didn't need to go back home. Georgia had made a reservation for him at a hotel near the museum which would mean that he could easily walk back and forth to the station and the museum.

Scott popped over to the ticket machine at Camden Town tube station. Inserting his debit card into the slot he rushed downstairs to the platform where a train was just a few minutes from the station. This was his first professional assignment and he was determined for it to go as smoothly as it comes. Desperate for the train to pull in, he almost panicked the waiting. Suddenly he felt the tiniest of sound and wind in his ears. Scott's super sensitivity could pick up the smallest bits of detail that he didn't like the smallest sounds more than the big bangs.

The train pulled into the station and Scott got up close as possible to the rush hour crowd. Kindly enough he let the people off the train, but carefully bustled onboard without grabbing attention. 'Come on, come on!' he whispered. 'Why did I have to pick the rush hour to get to York? Perhaps that deadline has caught up with me.' Scott couldn't get the hang of patience; his restlessness often made him run before he walked. This mental energy was better channelled elsewhere. So he started to put his hands on his face and count slowly. When planning it was vital for him to get it right, so he had to structure his routine accordingly.

As the train got going Scott was thinking that maybe he should've got on a later train. In an effort to avoid the sweat from the crowded carriage. *Nevertheless I just want the job done and dusted.*

Scott had got a place in the third carriage from the front, the most likely place to get a seat. But the seats were all occupied as it was so Scott found himself standing all the way to the next station. But still at least he managed to find a newspaper that had been left behind. Picking up disused newspapers was a commodity that Scott always likes to put them on a platform bench wherever he went giving other commuters something to read. Much to the astonishing confusion of other passengers!

Scott checked his watch, the digital display was 8.32. Still reeling with frantic activity Scott tried to concentrate his imperishable imagination on the paper. The front page was an old headline for a joyous nation from the other day when Arsenal won the Premier League three days ago. Both he and Auntie Jackie were jumping up and down for joy. The headline was like opening up into the pages of history as if Scott had discovered a time machine and an opportunity to revisit a really good time in his life. The past days of the well-being of his person made him feel whole and healthy. There are moments in his life that he wished he could have changed when he had a way of taking control of his destiny which was denied him. He was dismayed at the way people expected him to excessively indulge in his privileges as a disabled person. *Some people prefer it that I play the part of a hopeless, useless spastic. A poorly weak feeble creature with a soft head so manky they could squeeze me like a toy. If only I could show off my courage and strength to a person then they would see just what I am capable of. They seem only interested in disablement as a form of oppression. I can't stand it, I want to be seen as a strong warrior of justice that can teach the world how to be a better place.*

As he got to the massive King's Cross station, Scott got the hang of this new day. His luck had changed; it was a time of jubilation but not for despair of politics. He left the Northern Line and headed for the Piccadilly Line platform. The way around the station to get there was quite long, eventually passing the Hammersmith and City Line along the way. It was like an underground maze, than an Underground Tube station.

He checked his watch again making it 8.47, as he made it to the main terminus of the Kings Cross station building. The station was magnificent as Scott clasped his eyes on it for the first time. It looked like a cathedral to the London and North Eastern Railway, which Scott had long dreamed of travelling on. But that network no longer existed. He might not be travelling up North today but he dreamed that he might get the chance. *One day I'll be on the line to York, better late than never.*

Scott went back down to the Piccadilly Line making his way to take the train to Covent Garden for the Transport Museum. As he made his way there he thought about the history of King Cross station.

King's Cross was a grand tourist attraction, he thought as he went into the mall. *It had a long history dating back to 1851. I wonder what kind of things it had within these walls here. Perhaps I can find my own magical express to a wizardry world!*

He checked his watch again making it 9.15, as he made it to the Piccadilly Line platform. The overhead display revealed the next train would be along in one minute. The time was taken by enjoying some thinking time. A practice that often took away Scott's concentration of where he was. He was like a walking encyclopaedia that had a sight projecting his innovations in motion from a rocket to a high speed car.

Scott positioned where at the back of the second carriage, just as the train pulled into the station. Clambering aboard Scott got his journal out of his massive jacket pocket. It was something he had expanded on his coat to make his journalism gadgets a lot more mobile without the need to carry a bag around. This was something June didn't like, as she didn't approve of her son's initiative in radical circumstances. Scott flicked it open to his last entry to see where he had picked up inspiration from. The last thing he had written was from a trip to the science museum. However he hadn't put much pen to paper from that occasion. 'Right.' he said. 'Let's see if I can be a little bit more documenting this time.' The train boasted onwards into the tunnel like a speeding mole. The people cluttered around Scott wasn't really a problem for him. Unlock the everlasting complaints of his family, who don't care much for policy complaints, he took this naturally as the rush hour was supposed to be.

The train was at least half a minute out from Kings Cross. Scott's journal slipped out of his hands. As his odd posture fitted his autistic way of exhaustion he bent down, clumsily ending up on his knees.

THEN...

Scott's position was serendipity. As he was kneeling he was showered by hot shockwaves from the front of the train. The people to down the front were knocked down like dominoes acting like a break to the blast. Scott hardly felt distressed at the huge force that blew at him. Whereas most people would find this scenario unbearable Scott appeared very stoic to his present conditions. In the first few minutes he felt cold for comfort. *No way can I be comatose by this. I might be born feeble, but I've coped to better my feebleness.*

It took Scott a while to get a grip on himself, during which he felt entirely retarded from head to toe. His super sensitive nostrils were alight with the aroma of the burning metal and rubber. His vision was partially impaired by the thick black acrid smoke that was fuming inside the train. Waving the smoke aside and brushing his jacket. Then he instantly felt wet blood on his hands. He gazed at the stains noticing that he had been smeared in the remnants of the people that used to be standing around him. Standing up on his own two feet he looked upon his new surroundings. Overhead the lights were burnt out with some of the bulbs hanging loose from the ceiling while cables swung like loose intestines. The oppressive shockwaves had bent the handrails and torn a panel out of the ceiling. But worse still the passenger doors were blown off like emergency hatches exposing him to the live rails and the tunnel mounted cables. The entire interior had become a furnace with double gazed windows broken and shattered. The PVC flooring had been peeled like shredded floorboards. While the seats were fireproof they were stained in blood all patterned in the roots of a tree. It has become apparent that the train had been bombed!

While other people antagonised in thriving and screaming, Scott was sweat stained with feverish panic. He shook his head before breathing heavily to cut out the fear factor. Looking down to get it off the chest he remembered what shirt he put on. It was a shirt that kept him from going mad every time he looked at it's big nice letters: KEEP CALM AND CARRY ON! Just as you'd expect to be told how to continue in your duty without fear and hostility.

Proactively Scott knew how to leap right from the clutches of this situation. Just when his early job prospects were bleaker than a Dickens's residence, he had just realised an even better news story. However he didn't understand empathy to take an interest in this incident. *Blimey, a terrorist atrocity fit for a top correspondence. I wonder. Could this have been a terrorist or a suicidal person intent on taking people with him. NO! That's unfair and selfish. I'm not a negative condescending person. But what about these people. I don't have to stand and stare, no thanks. Instead I'll use this as an opportunity to prove myself.* Still under heavy breath he felt fortunately immortal and advantageous as his disability made him. However if he himself could get a story fit for a front page, could he also put himself in the frame of that story to show how good his disability could make him?

Spasticus Autisticus Rides Again

At this time there is a question on the last chapter about what Scott Hardy could do to better himself and show people what he is capable of. In this situation he has an opportunity to show what he is capable of without being a victim as he has no injuries. The media often portrays disabled people with an image of suffering, incapable of participating in a challenge and pitiable. But they never really seem to ask the disabled themselves without relying on the person's carers and guardians. Always choosing to seek consultation from experts like medical professionals and psychologists. If they granted them an opportunity, then they'd accept it to show what they are capable of. As disabled people of mental health we often ask ourselves that question when we want to better ourselves.

 As a writer of a work of fiction you'd probably expect me to be a liberal thinking leftist as most people in the arts appear to be. The reason why they think like that is because as writers, artists and performers they come from a profession that teaches a form of liberty in which they can express themselves as a collective or individual against the status quo and the mainstream that they live in. I have based that on my own experience from living and working amongst the company of the theatre business and the science fiction community. It seems to be a way of life for one of the arts, media and culture where you have to be willing to talk down at authority to show your expressing your rights to freedom and the liberalisation of a group or person in society, as if you have a duty to use your talent for a common good. So if you associate yourself with government and big business, you are seen as a traitor or a spokesperson standing up for authority. This may explain why celebrities tend to promote issues of a caring nature like healthcare, housing, green politics, poverty, social justice, third world problems, human rights and civil liberties. But when they speak out in support about right wing and nationalist issues like crime, terrorism, corporate activities, government intervention, military action or patriotism then you are seen as a parasite that must be exterminated.

The arts and media are not strictly a platform for the left or socialist and liberal ideals. They are open to any kind of thinking and anyone can use their music, paintings, literature and films to express whatever politics they believe in. I am an autistic person I have right wing views and I don't think that only leftist ideals of disability are all there is to be heard. Although disability issues are presented as a liberal and leftist cause there are some disabled people who think they are only using their disablement as a fuel for their rhetoric and actions. Social justice warriors often prey on poverty and injustice as a way of promoting equality. But when they fight for change they don't bother to come up with constructive solutions for society. These patronising pathetic do gooders haven't got anything useful for society but just use these problems as a means to promote egoism and passivity.

When disability issues like autism are presented in the arts, most stories about disablement depict a person who is humble but struggling, awkward and difficult. They look like pathetic, pitiful creatures with no hope but to make light of their problems. That just makes me feel like people see me as insufferable, hopeless and useless. It's like being exploited by a circus host paraded before an audience like a sideshow freak. My story of a Baffling Unoriginal is a tale of an autistic man who likes to think of himself as a hero, a rebel with a cause to fight for a belief in his abilities and what his value is in giving to his country and society. It focuses on giving a positive message about autism and what we are capable of that people don't recognise.

My novella did not go down well with the disabled community who felt that I had created a piece that created a story that showed autism in a bad light. To them it was a story that made autism in a negative way as if I had made living with a disability as sadistic, revolting and in bad taste. Especially as the original edition sees him violently attack someone who torments him with her pestilential ideas of using liberties to allow him to shunt himself into isolation. This made some of them think that I was vilifying mental health and they didn't want to associate themselves with me or my creation. But that was never what I tried to do. I was a frustrated man desperate to have his voice heard and so I channelled my expressions through my work, which is something that most artists do when they write songs, poems and paint pictures. Van Gogh had a number of mental issues and used his pain and sorrow to fuel his creative juices into his work. Every writer and artist has got some of their own personal being like their thoughts and feelings integrated into their work and my autism and mental issues are within this novella.

I wrote this in all seriousness. My intention was to create a protagonist where his autism was being used against him to make him suffer in society and be shunted into obscurity, rather than be suffering because of his impairment. He was made to look like he was being oppressed by a patronising social justice warrior who believed he was no good for what he wants out of life. Like a slave being constrained to his impairment who refused to accept the way things were set out for him. Even I was in a similar situation like this at the time of writing the novella. I was a frustrated writer, struggling and unemployed looking for jobs in a disorganised manner. I had such a hard time that I started to turn my despair into a story for an exercise in a creative writing course. It went down so well with my tutor that I turned it into a full length novella, which was 'A Baffling Unoriginal'. I found writing the story to be a great exercise in self-expression and determinism. It was like an artist using his own life experiences to paint a picture and let his words flow through his work.

As we all know many artistic people like to write powerful tales of strength when they write about conquering overwhelming powers of oppression. With the way my novella tells the story of conquest it looks like as if that concept has been performed in bad taste. Years later I discovered that I was not the first person to write such a supposedly offensive piece of work about disablement. There is another disabled writer and artist just like me. His name is Ian Dury, a singer-songwriter from Upminster, Essex.

Dury was born in 1942 and at the age of seven he had contracted polio from a swimming pool in Southend on Sea during an epidemic which partly crippled him. He spent the next two years living in and out of a hospital for disabled children. Afterwards he was educated in his primary school years at Chailey Heritage Craft School in East Sussex. This was a school and hospital for disabled children which taught him a variety of trades which included cobbling and printing craftworks. At that time disabled children were seen as hopeless, hideous and revolting. There was virtually no sign of them in school or even playing out in public places. Mostly dismissed from the mainstream, they were expected to not have much chances of employment in a world where they had to learn certain trades for financial security. These trades were the only type of work they would have been seen doing because their lack of mobility meant they could only take low skilled jobs. Dury called Chailey 'a prison as well as a hospital' and his mother arranged for him to go to a grammar school after he'd finished his time there. Throughout his life he struggled to find a positive attitude to his disability because they saw him as useless and unproductive and deprived him of opportunities. A situation that I feel is the same place that I am in despite living in an age of equality and discrimination laws.

Dury refused to accept his disability as a death sentence and whilst he was there at Chailey he had been rebellious and disruptive. A film biography of his life shows just how much of a free spirit he was. Andy Serkis played Dury in this film called 'Sex and Drugs and Rock and Roll' and it shows how through his childhood he was a disabled person who wasn't a campaigner, but a fighter vying for control of his destiny. Unlike most films about disablement which seem to be full of tear jerking tales of romance and struggles with their impairments and their happiness of overcoming odds, this depicted disablement as a force to be reckoned with where Dury would often make jokes about his own disability. There are plenty of rude and amusing jokes about disablement throughout most of which come from Dury, as he did so in real life. He was pretty much a slave who was inspired to break the shackles of his disability where he declared that 'people like me do not want sympathy, they want respect!'. This is the part of his life where his music became a battle cry for the rights and liberties of disabled people across the world.

In 1981 the United Nations marked the 'International Year of Disabled Persons. This was supposed to be an opportunity for the disabled community to get equal opportunities, rehabilitation and prevention of disabilities. Ian Dury however saw this as counter-productive and patronising as if all the disabled people of his kind needed nothing but a welfare handout, a wheelchair and sympathy from the world's riches.

In response to this Dury released a song that had become one of his least known success stories. The song is called 'Spasticus Autisticus' and it's about a slave who was crying out for freedom. Dury described the song as 'a war cry' and has a remarkable tone to it's sound and lyrics and if we deconstruct it we can find some surprising revelations about how he felt as a disabled person.

Dury got the idea for the song's name and chanting chorus from the film 'Sparticus' which also tells the story of a slave, albeit in the Roman Empire. The repeated chant of "I'm Spasticus, I'm Spasticus, I'm Spasticus Autisticus" is similar to that of a scene in the film on the hillside after the battle where all the slaves inspired by their leader shout back at the Romans in solidarity 'I'm Sparticus', as a cry for their own space in society with no recrimination.

Other sections of the song revealed how Dury felt about disablement being taken for granted where the underscore of it was 'if you want to offer help then give them what they need, not what you need'. He was fed up with people from 'normal-land' putting 'peanuts in his tin' and to 'thank the Creator you're not in the state I'm in'.

One of the most peculiar lines is '54 appliances in leather and elastic, 100'000 thank yous from 27 spastics'. The meaning of this line refers to the time when disabled people were exploited to get them to make useless disposable items often made in leather and elastic for money from charities. It was an utterly outrageous practice that was wrong on so many levels. Apparently they had to earn the right to earn their welfare help because the practice was similar to community service. It made the disabled feel like as if they were being punished for a crime they did not commit, making them feel bad for having their impairment. Able-bodied people bought these items thinking they were helping disabled people and the disabled builders had to send thank you notes to them. It's not known if the money raised (if any) ever went to these disabled people though.

Although it was a powerful song with a strong message it wasn't accepted that way. It was declared to be in bad taste and full of some very offensive lyrics. The verses in the song had some derogatory terms used to describe disabled people. Specifically, the use of the word 'spastic' which is a provocative term to describe a disabled person, even though there was a charity for cerebral palsy called 'Spastics Society' at the time. One of the most notable lines is "I dribble when I piddle, cos my middle is a riddle" which refers to the way some disabled people appear to be with mobility impairments. These lines along with the rest of the lyrics are what led to the BBC and several other radio stations banning it from airplay. It was so badly received that there was no sign of it in the charts.

 Despite Dury's intentions some people felt that he was exaggerating the negative aspects of being disabled. But he insisted that it was about an enslaved person whose pride shall know no boundaries or limitations in an explanatory way. I like the song as a disabled person and a music fan and I think Spasticus should be a rallying cry for justice with a call to make the world a fairer place where I share a space with normal people and not be shunted into a place of everlasting care. Ironically at the London 2012 Paralympic Games opening ceremony 'Spasticus Autisticus' was performed by the band Orbital and members of the Graeae Theatre Company. It was received as a powerful battle cry for civil justice as displayed by the performers as the whole crowd applauded them for portraying disablement with dignity and courage.

 'Spasticus Autisticus' isn't a charity song, it's an anti-charity song coming from a charity recipient who wants something better than having money thrown to him for food and warmth. If you think I as a mental health person who resents charitable donations out of the many millions of other disabled people who accept charity as an ungrateful person, then maybe you should go and ask those who receive handouts. Ian Dury and I are not the only people who feel that we are being exploited for fundraising and political issues endorsed for capital gain, there are plenty of them across the world and in the disability communities across the world. The problem with the situation that the disabled suffer that others try to better for them is that they are being fought by the wrong people. These people are not politicians, lawyers or humanitarians, but social justice warriors. These are perhaps the worst and most futile of activists ever known. A long time ago they used to be promoters of socially progressive ideas. Now they are irritating negative people who chant politically correct views in the name of social liberalism and inclusiveness that reflects a warped view of a dystopia like that of Aldous Huxley's Brave New World. I don't trust them to stand up for the community of autism yet alone social issues that affect me because they have no power or responsibility that makes them an effective weapon. The former socialist

Frederick Hayek said of social justice that it is a meaningless conception which believes that 'the state should treat different people unequally in order to make them equal'. That means certain ethnic groups, minorities and cultures should be treated differently to the mainstream, hence why we have inequality to whites and blacks, rich and poor, lower and middle class. So it isn't even compatible with liberal ideas.

Ever since the world of celebrity became politically active poverty has become an industry that the wealthy elite in politics, business and the arts use to drive consumerism and excess. To them poverty and in particular the disabled community are useful as an instrument for the cult of celebrity to sell their brand and image. They use the concept of social justice for their own meaningless tirades towards things that don't agree with their liberal elitist views. In the eyes of social justice warriors and liberal celebrities charity is a platform for selling their ideas and products like a fashion statement. Consider the BBC Children in Need charity which raises money for causes which include children with autism.

In 2014 it was found that Children in Need had a £87 million held in an investment portfolio made from donations made over the years. They say that this is due to the fact that they give out donor money in instalments rather than lump sums to the projects it supports. This charity has had an annual telethon on the BBC since 1980 with a host of famous celebrities endorsing the charity which has raised money through the purchasing of records, books and other merchandising with the proceeds going to the charities. But the amount of money raised isn't always channelled to the right people. An independent charity watchdog called Intelligent Giving found that in 2006 the charity had raised £33 million of which £2.4 million was used for administration costs.

I have got friends in the arts and media and I have watched them care passionately for the charitable causes that they support out of the liberal arts where they work. I am happy for them to raise money and commit to volunteer work with refugees, the poor and the disabled. But as a former charity recipient I have my criticisms about the way they cherry pick who they help and how they do it. I'm sure it's a great and noble cause but the people in these situations don't like being treated as beggars when they have their dignity still intact. They don't want sympathy they want something better for themselves. Charity recipients who get into the public eye can become more poor than they were before.

 Birhan Woldu was of the survivors of the 1984 famine in Ethiopia and became the poster girl for the Live Aid concert's mission to feed the victims. Years later when she was all grown up Woldu found herself unemployed because of her association with a western charity that continued to portray her country in an image of despair. While Live Aid's founder Sir Bob Geldof has gone onto make a name for himself off the back of his charity work. Geldof started off as a lead singer of a band called the Boomtown Rats, which at the time of the Ethiopian Famine had faded into obscurity. He had a reputation for being a foul mouthed, insufferable, trouble maker. This is hardly the qualities of a charity entrepreneur and he isn't really a good character amongst the aid industry neither. Yet he still continues to preach his politics without any regards to the impact he is having. Some African leaders have asked him to step down from the anti-poverty movement because his economic illiteracy and pretentious ego is leaving them with more debt than development. That is not the right way to fight poverty.

Activism is about fighting for change through constructive and progressive action, not a means to promote a problem with a passive ego. Using the poor and the disabled like this is like that of a homeless street urchin being taken into the company of a showman. Putting him on display like a circus freak with the public throwing money in his tin that only amounts to peanuts. If I was in that position I would throw the peanuts in the face of the imitation social justice warrior and then take the tin to gorge his eyes out.

At the time of writing I was watching a debate on TV about how celebrities get involved in political issues. As a disabled person, whose welfare is promoted by these famous people, I think they should try looking at what exactly they are letting themselves in for by associating themselves with these charities. Instead of it being about raising money and fighting for social justice they are using poverty, disablement, climate change and political issues for publicity purposes and promoting their careers using the charities as a stage to sell tickets to watch them perform and sell their products. This is nothing more than orchestrated complacent compassion used to drive consumerism for the sake of the image of society and the celebrities involved. They believe that by associating charity with consumerism they are giving a voice to the helpless and making the concept of helping people a fun filled carnival so that they can boost funding for projects to aid the poor. But instead they are actually making a growth industry out of the poor and in order to make a profit out of that poverty and displacement they keep the poor from bettering themselves. This is just pure complacency and it is making the concept of helping others a dirty act of committing altruistic deeds.

There is a documentary that explores these social issues called 'Poverty Inc'. It reveals how the practice of tackling poverty for the last 30 years hasn't worked. Among some of the reasons behind this is the way that famous people use the power of compassion and sympathy to make the charity's money. Money which mostly goes onto fund the charity's administration costs and projects to help the poor. This is something that anti-capitalists say is an example of western richness exploiting the poor for publicity. One strong statement that Poverty Inc. uses to describe the world aid system is from a quote by the 15th century Italian philosopher Niccolo Machiavelli: 'The reason that there will be no change is because those who stand to lose from change have all the power. Those that stand to gain from change have none of the power'. This is where the flaw in the cult of these liberal philanthropists stands. They have no power or responsibility for the problems that they address and therefore their constant preaching of their politics and compassion is insignificant. All their politics represents is an infantilization of political affairs and social issues. They may cry out for change but they don't fight for the freedom of the poor to become independent of aid.

The problem with famous people in the arts who endorse charities is that there is virtually no accountability for their kind-hearted actions. These celebrities have got access to a protection racket of public relations executives and lawyers to protect their image. One thing about those who they help is that they can silence them in a carefully crafted way. They often collaborate with the charities so that they can hide any lack of progress in their fundraising activities from the public eye. One example of this is how the majority of celebrities endorse charities for sick and impoverished people in developing countries like Africa and Asia. Some people think that they are short changed and left out by the way they spend their riches on some people that are not native to them. It's not just because of the publicity they can get, it's also with lack of accountability. If the concept of a famine relief charity concert was to raise money in Britain the recipients of the charity can publicly give feedback with ease as they are in position to get access to the media and the charity bosses who are giving them this money. So if they have a problem with the money and aid they are receiving they are in a position to complain and the fundraisers will have to answer to them. But in the far off places like Africa and Asia where there is a lot of poverty and lack of access to communication they wouldn't be able to question the source of their handout. Birhan Woldu came to Britain to demonstrate the work of Live Aid from a charity recipient's point of view in 2005 and as it happens she had never heard of the musicians involved in the charity record or the concert. There is no distribution of their music to these countries and the same goes for people in the other arts as well where western film stars are virtually unheard of and they don't know what they are letting themselves in for in receipt of their charity. So they are hopelessly made to look helpless and it drowns out the other side of Africa. An Africa that I can relate to as I have a great wealth of skills in creativity, enterprise and innovation.

These Africans don't deserve to be excluded from the campaign for change. Like me with my autism they are not stupid and incapable of sustaining their own livelihood. They can save their own people through collaboration with western enterprise and government for development funds. During the EU referendum campaign, of which I was a Leave activist, I felt my own abilities were being ignored so that these elite supporting celebrities can protect their image and their reputation. They were much more interested in exhibiting their humanitarian causes for publicity than giving the poor the tools to create their own livelihood. By promoting the poverty and injustice of society only, they are ignoring the abilities of those they help and denying them their right to let their creativity flourish. It's just the same as keeping a second hander in his place as described by Howard Roark in 'The Fountainhead', a novel by Ayn Rand.

Philanthropy, which was once the noble and honourable purpose of gifting aid to the poor through charity, has now become a multi-billion-dollar franchise of the wealthy metropolitan liberal elite through entertainment and corporate sponsorship. The current model for aid and support for the poor including the disabled and mental health isn't working and it needs to change. Although I am a capitalist I don't accept unethical wealth creation that thinks that some people are more deserving than others that the person giving the aid has to feel good in his part of giving that the recipient of the aid has to accept it on the giver's terms. So if a mental health person receives money from charity to afford food and warmth to stay alive then the position of the person is being taken advantage of unfairly. But if the mental health person has a gift to give to the world that can better his position and receives charity to better himself then that person has received the seeds of change that blossom to make the world a better and happier place.

In the years that I have been an activist for autism I have found that some people think they know better about dealing with social and economic problems better than those who deal with the battles themselves. These are the so called luvvies, famous liberals who use their celebrity status to denounce populism and criticism of their ideas in the name of civil liberties and social justice. They have a habit of making comments about the general consensus in a guilt free judgemental manner regardless of their lack of knowledge and condescension towards those they criticise. Even though they are likely to upset those who are affected by their comments that could ruin their business as a performer. These luvvies are part of a branch of the metropolitan liberal elite that represent a new type of class division between social-liberalism and national conservatism. This makes the luvvies insufferable to listen to especially as they accuse their critics of being economically illiterate, uncaring, racist or despicable. I don't trust them or their charity to speak up for mental health yet alone social justice. Most of them have never read a book on a political philosophy or studied a problem in real detail that affects the lives of millions to make any show themselves as saviours of mental health.

One thing that is controversial in these luvvies' support of charities is how they cherry pick the causes they support. Most of them never really do it out of compassion and sympathy but out of publicity for their own careers. They become complacent when they face the backlash against them thinking they are more intelligent than ordinary people that don't deserve to criticise them. This is a dangerous mix of business and pleasure and it may endanger their careers. Welsh actor Micheal Sheen gave his support to saving a special needs facility at a primary school in Monmouthshire by simply backing an online petition in January 2016. A month before that there was a flooding disaster in West Yorkshire and there was outcry at the lack of funds available for the need to build and improve flood defences. The big charities were brought into question about the choices of who they were helping and not giving any of their funds to the flood victims. There was also criticism about the UK's foreign aid budget of $12 billion not being diverted to help the flood victims. Sheen denounced this criticism as an ideological agenda and that he was 'sick' of hearing from the people who were affected by the floods whose plight was being used as part of a 'false argument'. This is not just a case of hypocrisy it is an example of a privileged person dictating the needs of the suffering. I can relate to this as a mental health person who has his own needs and care judged by experts in the field of sociology and psychology who are more in communication with authority members rather than the actual people that need their help.

Anti-consumerist groups claim that the whole purpose for celebrities to endorse charities like those that help people with autism is just for getting people to buy their products. A North Korean state made documentary demonstrates this using a number of famous people as examples. The documentary is actually a film commissioned by the North Korean government to tell in their words 'how the western world uses propaganda to subvert the people into submission'. One of these is the cult of celebrity and it discredits their credibility in a demonic way but it clearly points out the flaws in the way celebrities misuse poverty for promoting good causes to charity.

According to the documentary there are other ways in which they can help the poor, which indeed there are, but wouldn't do much good for their careers. Consider Madonna a famous musician who adopted an African boy from Malawi in 2006 and then later a girl in 2009. Around the time of the second adoption Madonna's home country of the United States had a big case of poverty of it's own that she could have presented to highlight at home. About 13.2 % of Americans live in poverty with 1.5 million on less than $2 a day. Not to mention that there are also more than 1.5 million homeless children in America and that figure is still rising. Yet for some reason a celebrity like a famous musician chooses to adopt from a foreign country because it generates better publicity for herself. You probably won't get that kind of publicity if you took in and helped one of your own. The PR strategy behind this is that if you go for the poorest you look the most caring, and the more caring you appear the more publicity you get.

This is a prime example of collaborating with corporations to make out of helping the poor. Such actions like this made me question the value of the charity that I receive and henceforth I don't approve of charitable causes. Why should I trust my case to a famous entertainer who treats his politics like a fashion statement? Making a show out of a person's despair like turning a poor street urchin or a disabled homeless man like an amusing creature to be put on display to be carted around the world like a circus freak. Sympathy like that can put right off showing your generosity and make you feel loathing towards yourself and shame on the showman. The leftist do not have a monopoly on compassion, the right are just as caring as they are. The major difference is how the problem is addressed. The left use showmanship to promote the problem and create victimhood, whilst the right use creativity and intelligence to solve the problem. To make a real impact on autism getting to better itself I need the power, not just the money to make something of myself.

In keeping with the spirit of Spasticus Autisticus these charity recipients deserve a better way of life through the giving of opportunities, not welfare. We need to rethink autism right now. I have a deep connection to the song and I have taken Spasticus Autisticus as the soundtrack of my struggle. As a tribute to Ian Dury as Spasticus I have written a poem honouring his spiritual guidance.

Spasticus Austicus the great rebel of the realm
A slave who rallies for escape from hell.
The masters do not care for our ideas
only our being in the state it's in.
Makes them take pity, which we don't want
as if we are worthless, but we are indeed strong

Our pride shall not be institutionalised
with no part to play, no role or place
for our part supposedly meaningless.
The standards of care are no use with a clueless pig,
who bully and beat us unto our own limitations.
We will beat them until they trotter on and realise their
own faults.

Cry out in anger at the injustice towards us,
the pathetic useless do gooders,
who nothing of our despair and discontent.
We are better than they are,
they can stick their charity where the sun don't shine.
Their trinkets are tokens of wastage.

Take direction into greatness,
Your impairment maybe a blessing.
Autisticus has autism, a powerful force
That should be reckoned with.

God created us unequal to normal land
For a purpose to build a better world that everyone
deserves.

Stupid appliances, no thank you.
No one expects second class standards,
Accept our thinking instead for success in science or art.

Rise and fight fellow rebels in tribute to our own follower,
Almighty Spasticus Autisticus.
I'm no bloody retard!
I'm no bloody retard!
Who says normal land is any better,
For I don't feel any better from patronising services of the masters.

CHAPTER SIX

Scott was unhurt but a strong aroma of burning metal, rubber and flesh hung in the air. Heavily aware that there was someone on the floor moving close to him and thriving in agony, but Scott's social interaction had negligence. Out of touch with recognising a person's feelings. To Scott this man was acting out in a way that he couldn't read the expressions on his face. However based on his previous experiences he could tell that the man was in pain. As he remembered back to his early years when he got hit and by the ways he is being made to suffer from petty domestics. He clicked his fingers trying to snap into social connectivity. *Come on! Come on!* Without considering the other people screaming, at least they were unable to pay attention to what he was doing. 'Right a bombed train, people dead, dying or suffering. I can smell burning everywhere. They need help...Oh God I hate this side of me!'

Scott went over to turn the man and put him upright sitting against a bent pole from the floor. 'Are you okay?' asked Scott. His weak prosody sounded even more oddly stressed towards his feelings for this person. However from what he saw he was overly formal. 'No that's a stupid question; I can tell you're in a bad way.'

'I knew I should've caught that first one quicker.' said the stranger. 'What's with that about a stupid question?'

'It's nothing really.' he replied. 'I'm just autistic. But its okay, I'm not as weak as I should be disabled.' Scott surveyed the man's ashen stained clothing. The soot from the one hundred and fifty year old tunnels had shuddered off during the blast. Shockwaves at such a volume like that would've showered it through the both ends of the tunnel. 'Well if they were decent enough to understand they would know about this now.'

'What, what did you say?'

'Oh nothing.' flustered Scott. 'I'm just somewhat...well you wouldn't understand me for all the time I'll probably be with you 'til we get out.'

'How's my leg?' said the man.

'It's like a freshly butchered animal.' said Scott. The man's leg had a portion of flesh severed from the lower limb. He couldn't see it but Scott could tell that the fabric had gone with the shrapnel's flesh damage. 'Or at least looking inside it.' Before he went any further Scott felt an introduction would be wiser. 'I'm Scott by the way.' Already an advantage had come in use here. Although he felt disturbingly panicked but his tone suggests bravery.

'Well that's nice to know your name.' he said. 'I'm Nick.' Nick held out to shake his hand with Scott. Quite an extraordinarily British thing to do. 'I always thought I had a funny pair of legs.'

'They are not funny.' stated Scott. 'There just...Oh I see. Sorry, I don't get jokes like that. I just take things literally sometimes. Just when I thought I had got over that sort of thing years ago.'

'Well at least you're lucky to be in one piece.' said Nick thoughtfully. 'I've now got a disability and I don't think you need another one.'

'But I bet it would make an interesting collection.' Scott joked. He looked around for a moment as he took off his coat. Scott found a cool jagged piece of the damaged train. Slicing the sleeve of his coat, he then returned to Nick. Wrapping the piece of clothing around his badly damaged leg. 'Right hold that there for a minute, while I tear another bit of my coat.' Nick did so while Scott returned to cutting another piece of his coat.

'What are you doing with a coat?' asked Nick.

'Cutting it, what do you think!'

Nick gave a confused cough. 'Erm, oh yeah your...artistic aren't you.' 'Autistic. That's with a U not an R.' Scott explained.

'Sorry, err why have you brought a coat out with you in the first place on a warm day, I mean?' Scott then realised what he was actually trying to say.

'Well that's a thing I've got about mixing in with other trends.' Said Scott.

'Trends?'

'Yes, like wearing shirts in summer and scarves in winter and all.'

'I see.' Scott got back to Nick by wrapping the other cropped sleeve and combined it with the other strip of fabric into a tourniquet.

'How's that?' said Scott. 'Can you feel your leg at all?'

'No.' said Nick. 'It's probably paralysed as well.'

'Well it's not too bad.'

'How can you even say that?'

'Listen, I've got by incredibly well in life using my disability to it's given me some strong abilities. But you know what, you're the first person whose ever given me a chance to prove it.' Nick smiled as Scott gestured he'd finally found self-futility.

Just as the screaming continued Scott found himself a saviour in an apocalypse. They only wanted to be free, to be out of here, to reach safety and get back home or into intensive care. They were trapped 100ft below ground and there wasn't an exit for 457 metres from the next station. *It's gonna take time before anyone from above is aware that the train has been rocked off the rails. Oh, well. At least I'm in the middle of it entitling myself to the title of a priceless voluntary work. My ideas are useful to these people and I think they will appreciate it.* 'So come on, you've been yapping all the time. Just get on with it!'

'Yeah, I know.' said Nick. 'It's madness just doing nothing.'

'Sorry about that Nick, I was just in me own...never mind.' said Scott. 'If you'll excuse me, I've got other people to help out.' Scott trod seriously onwards as maddening anxiety ran through his blood. Anxiety was his driving force behind his obsessions that he could not let go until it was over. All he needed to go on was just a set situation to divulge his panic into relief.

Scott walked across to the front of the carriage. Just before his curiosity took him to the door frame there was a man fearfully shaking and trembling. As Scott touched him on the shoulder the man flipped out violently. Scott unable to understanding his expressive feelings could only look upon his aggressive fright. 'Tell me, what are you feeling?' *No wait. Another interaction trouble.* 'I mean are you hurt or is that blood all over your body someone else's blood.' No response. Instead just pushed past Scott. Like a headless chicken just stormed to the back of the train flinging doors open. *Bloody coward! I've seen people act more comical than Corporal Jones.*

Scott turned to continue his observation of the door frame. The explosion had practically ripped the entire wall adjacent to the carriage in front of it. The frame of the carriage left no door to open but to just walk right through it. *Tube train carriage access doors open inwards, the blast must've ripped it right from it's hinges.* He carefully navigated the jagged wreckage. Mindful of the creaks and grinding sensations with every step, he was trying to be careful not to trap himself.

The path filled a burning sensation haunting his past. Back in his schooldays Scott may have been a "memory man" as described by June. But this supposed gift had a difficulty for him to be accepted by his classmates. *They might have ignored me but I haven't got to bother with them. I stuck me self in the library or else walk around the playground listening to my imaginative conscious in motion. God help it I just don't like going about with them. Thank God I dropped out of that Godforsaken cattle farm.* Conscious about isolation he'd stay at home after school and never bothered to know about people. Digesting information on philosophy, trains and alternative ideas to the way they lived. The other kids saw his habits as a means for a joke. *Stupid morons happily enslaved to their liberties they wouldn't bother to fight for a power struggle.* At one time he tried to interact with them, showing them how intelligent he was. But their behaviour spurned on him when he couldn't fit in. It was quite embarrassing and eventually he tried suicide. But he didn't go for it because he was too stubborn to give in. *I told that old bag. Why does she never listen to me? I've seen families with disabled children try better to make their children succeed instead of making them end up as hopeless, useless spastics. Okay now, my chance is here. Now I must prove myself and show them how acceptable I am.* When frustrated Scott's absorbed knowledge led him to think negatively about himself, he found alternative ways by obsessing about something positive. Exercising his imagination was perhaps his best quality and an advantage to that end. Now that he was here in this very train disaster, it meant that he could put that knowledge into labour. After all he was a train enthusiast and a great read of instruction manuals. He understood the basics of first aid and how to navigate around a train's structural components. With that in mind Scott could improvise on his own without supported care.

CHAPTER SEVEN

Scott motioned carefully where the damage had been done between the two carriages. Looking straight ahead he could just make out the crater, where to his best guess the bomb had once been. Scott had a lifelong appetite for rational thinking. It's a compatible feature of Aspergers syndrome that Scott used to argue for the right logic. *An eye for the smallest details can be incredibly useful. As for the bomb's trigger, that couldn't have been left onboard. Someone would steal it for it's valuables only to be blown up. This has got to be a suicide bomber, he couldn't blow it from a radio signal as it's underground. But after 7/7 a suicide bomber wouldn't try again this instantly. It would probably be from something else that would be vulnerable.*

Scott felt like he'd landed in a different country. Venturing to this place was perhaps his most toughest challenge and this is where he needed to make connect himself. He couldn't just ignore it and even though he struggled to connect with people socially he had an opportunity to connect with these people now. *I can now understand what kind of suffering goes on when the bent pratts are in charge! POLITICAL CORRECTNESS. It's going to be the death of us as it is when the liberal fascists tell us how to think. It's not foreigners who are the problem, it's the system that teaches us that we should not take any responsibility for our own care. They think I can't think, and that I am incapable of working.* Scott thought such an unthinkable act of terrorism like this long gone since the last attack. But there would be something about this tragedy that made it different from a conventional terrorist attack. *My ways of taking a literal interpretation of things brings spots of déjà vu and irony. It's tricky enough for me to overcome that part of my condition.*

A woman, just woken up from the blast, was the first person to come to Scott's attention. Spitting bits out from where she was lying on the peeled plastic matted floor. As she wiped the debris away she found herself in wet burns. Scott hurried over to her dimly lit body, a momentarily flickering light above showed her clothes stained in burns. The woman didn't move nor even speak. Scott wiped his fingers on the shiny liquid that drenched her suit. Opposite him where she was sitting was a broken laptop. An expensive thing Scott was compulsive not to purchase because of his preserved warmth in his bank account. There was liquid from the LCD screen spilling out from where the pixels were projected. *Oh yes, that stuff burns when you get it over you. The dead owner must've been using it. Her burns are probably going spasms now.*

Just above him Scott noticed a shattered window had an arm in the gesture of trying to climb back in. As he pulled the arm it turned out to be just a single limb. *From one of those poor souls mutilated in the blast.* Surrounding was full dead as it appeared. The explosion had scattered body parts over the floor and the seats. Limbs, organs and charred remains made the scene look like something out of a no holds barred war movie.

He looked down at the injured woman noticing her badly wounded right arm. Scott kneeled down to get a closer look. 'Who are you then?' Her muffled voice made her barely able to talk. He brushed aside the bits of debris to get a better look at her. *They're must be some twenty - thirty people in pieces here.* 'With her so close it's a miracle she survived at all.' whispered Scott. He looked around to see if anyone else was moving. The darkness made it difficult to see if anyone who wasn't blasted to pieces was just dead from shock or fright. *Maybe I should just stick with this one.* He returned to the injured woman.

It required a slap from Scott to bring her round. When this happened. 'You just hit me!' A surprising reaction no doubt.

'Well of course.' explained Scott. 'It's part of the procedure. Some people like you need encouragement like that.'

'Alright then.' she said, abruptly. 'I'll make sure I'll remember it. That should be in the report when I bring the case.' The woman had a strong demure motherly like quality to gratitude. It wasn't trauma but she had a grovelling and self-depreciating manner.

'I'll say...there's plenty of it around here to prove what's happened to us.' Scott looked at her face. Just for a second he was experiencing one of his visual flashbacks. Had he seen this woman from someplace before?

'Who are you by the way?'

'Glouster. Jane Glouster.' she said.

'Jane Glouster. I've heard of that name from somewhere before. Jane Glouster...Glouster...where do I know that name?' Right now was all that mattered so Scott didn't have to think about past. But the name Glouster was now on his mind as he tried to remember who this woman was. *Of course Jane Glouster, the wicked witch of Gloucestershire. She was involved in the trial of a mentally ill man who was refused justice because of Glouster's evidence in which she used his mental health against him.* 'The evil witch, I'd really like to cast a spell on her demonic clients.'

With Jane coughing for the smoke at her mouth he looked around for another bit of clothing. She covers her mouth with a hanker chief from her jacket pocket. Suddenly there was a flicker going all round them as Scott peered through the broken window frames for all to see. Ahead and behind them the emergency lights came on. 'No wonder why the blast was concentrated. This is a narrow single track train line.'

Having found a scarf, he began to wrap it around Jane's talking all the way through the procedure. 'All the other train lines are double tracked, which would've deflected the blast to an even wider degree.'

'That's hardly important at this hour.' said Jane. 'Whoever was involved in this must have been out to get someone. It looks like I've got a good opportunity here to make some fat load of cash. I tell you I owe this guy. I'll be famous if I take this case.'

'You filthy profiteer.' said Scott in cursed way. 'This disaster is something that has caused a tragic loss of life. If you see this as nothing but a business opportunity, then they are going to want to be hunt you down. Justice is totally out of place these days thanks to a mix of liberties and human rights gone wrong. Whose side is that system on anyway?'

'Well at least the people behind it were unaware that they could use it.' said Jane. 'Now all that matters is seeing what we need to do is right for the people here. I think if they followed my prerogative then no harm will come to them. I am right about everything, because I was there. This will be the biggest judgement anyone has ever made.'

'Well I'm not really interested in your psychotic rants now, so I think I'll go over there and make myself useful. Thanks.' Said Scott.

Discarding from her aid he looked deeper for other casualties. Scott wasn't really much interested in discussing political matters with people who act in a one sided way. But he was very outspoken about them, and sometimes in a way that is only described in a one-way communication. Every Sunday he'd get the morning paper there was just a lot of nonsense in them that angered him and left his distressed. *Maybe if the courts were better then I can pick one up without reading about criminal victories. Those lawyers for the likes of her are maniacal mothers of ignorance and an immoral bankrupt disgusting carcass. She even looks evil with her Cruella like eyesight.*

'What about the rest of me?' said Jane. 'Are my injuries serious in any way?'

'No.' *But it'll be much simpler if you were dead you political farce.* Scott was happy to help out, but to this one. He was more interested in her moral character. He decided to try and tempt her to see how negative she could be. 'Are you by any chance involved in the law?'

'Why do you need to know?' she abruptly asked.

'You look very familiar to me.' Said Scott. 'I've seen you in a story in a paper a while ago...wait, wait a minute. I think I know now.'

'You think you know what? If so are you sure?' said Jane. 'I think your crazy and disturbing. I've dealt with people of your condition before. You an aspie, you shouldn't be in a position to help me.'

'Never mind the political toss. I can't stand it.' Scott's mind clicked into operation and as soon as he knew it: 'Now I know, Jane Glouster, you were the one who got that bipolar sufferer out of work and away from his employment. YOU'RE A HUMAN RIGHTS LAWYER!'

'Yes, that's right.' she replied. Scott wasn't traumatised, motivated by madness. The idea of coming across a human rights lawyer in this position was a prospect that Scott had long been anticipating.

'Oh thank God for that. Oh fantastic, the law has finally entered the battlefield. The great human protector of justice. How does it feel when you now know your petty defence laws can't protect the real people or even you?'

'Stay away from me you crazy bastard.' Retorted Jane.

'I'm not a psychopath, I'm a high functioning mental health person with a strong mind and a will to defeat ableism. Tell me Jane, how does it feel to see disablement with ableness?'

Just then someone from beside Scott coughed himself awake. A bloody ashen Asian man with weak lungs grasped his inhaler to his mouth. Unable to compress it Scott had to take it from his fragile hands and do it for him. 'Are you okay?' The man gripped his aide's arm, which made Scott react in a childlike manner. Or at least that's how he used to when he couldn't stand being touched by girls in his schooldays. He didn't like getting his skin in contact with strangers so he shoved them aside. But he had learnt to embrace being touched as he reached twenty. His super sensitive palms had become helping hands.

'They've got me once again.' said the man with his thick Asian accent that Scott could barely understand. 'How did they find me?'

'What's that supposed to mean?' asked Scott impatiently. 'Did you know what this is all about?' he started to shake him up. 'What is it, what is it?'

'Those terrors from Bangladesh have come back to drag me to hell with them.' he replied in a delirious way.

'Bangladesh! You're from Bangladesh!' said Scott, before turning to Jane. 'You see Jane. This man fled from Bangladesh, but now it looks like liberties for everyone who don't share the same brains. Even I don't share the same brains as you. Are you satisfied with having them run amok,'

'I haven't got long.' said the dying man, interrupting Scott. Then he pulled Scott's ear to his mouth. 'Please don't let her get away again.'

'What do you mean?'

'My name is Tariq Khan.' He gasped for air. 'I was with the man who set the bomb off. I was his social worker and psychiatrist. His name was Frank Craine. They missed the signs and let him go off.'

'Frank Craine, you mean the man with bipolar who lost his job to the chemical company?' asked Scott. 'I didn't think he'd hoard a stash of chemicals from his work place.'

'He didn't, he actually took an experimental explosive from them a year before he lost his job. I thought I could stop him. We were following her to the High Court to get a retrial. Frank must have spotted her and take a chance to stop her.'

'By killing her with a factory-made bomb?' said Scott. 'That would be nice, but I wouldn't go that far to get revenge. Killing does more of a disservice and it makes the idiots like her use us as weapons against their opponents. I'm not a puppet of the liberal elite to be used for political actions.'

Bleeding very freely Tariq eclipsed his life with a seizure from loss of blood. Angry Scott just wanted to scream out. He clenched his fists and held onto his composure. *Mental health really is stigmatised, this man should have been bettered respected by his community. That woman has done a real disservice to him by making him out to be a madman who has only got dark, disturbing thoughts on his mind.* Unlike the explosion that Frank Craine made, Scott had to be able to build a better understanding of mental health. He needed people to accept his best qualities. *Killing people out of anger with your mental health is bad. Fight your enemies with honour NOT scumbag yobbery!*

Despite a lack of empathy Scott did have a sense of condolences. He looked at where Craine had been stared intently. *Maybe I'm not an emotional person but I know what I 'am: Defiant, Rebellious and Intelligent.* 'Sorry they can couldn't provide well for you. But it just goes to show that no matter where you go no one has any concept or understanding of mental health. I really think that this is just negligence and undermining from people who think you deserve sympathy but not respect. There's not a place in the world for real equality, everyone just expects you to think the same about themselves. Ruthless and reckless.' Just as he turned enviously to Jane, she was now unconscious again. 'Poor pathetic woman, she really needs to see the consequences in ignorance.'

However idiosyncratic his lingo was he didn't care, as long he knew what he was talking about. Now he started to talking to Jane even if she wasn't listening. 'Like what's happened to Tariq there it's exactly what's happening to you. Your clients must be pleased.' His occasionally tedious verbal fluency estranged the melody of his speech. 'And what does that prove, Jane? Who exactly are you protecting: the human or the monster?'

Inequality is a fact of life: tolerate and accept all classes of citizens!

In the original story of 'A Baffling Unoriginal' which is now the first edition of this novella I set the train accident on the 7/7 bombings in London. At the time I wanted to experiment with a situation in which a person with autism would deal with a terrorist attack and explore the themes of disablement and race issues and the chaos and disorder brought upon by a bureaucratic social-liberalist government. But it wasn't properly received because the way that it had been written didn't seem original and even as it was a tale about an unoriginal autist the theme wasn't understood. It occurred to me that I hadn't really settled a case for autism as a force to reckoned with in this case. To make the case for autism with a voice to prove positive I had to show Scott as an active protagonist fighting for a cause for autism to be accepted into the mainstream. That's why I changed the bomber to that of a mentally ill man who was disturbed and dismissed by a society that was vilifying him because of his illness. It would be an opportunity for Scott Hardy to uncover the truth of his motives and henceforth show how for disablement to stand up for their rights they must use the positive aspects of their disability. Showing their strengths rather than their negative thoughts as if they are damned with discontent.

At the time of writing the novel in 2007 I had grown fed up with the way that disabled people where portrayed in the media. The majority of disabled characters in works of fiction at the time were pitied, pathetic and often downtrodden. Pictured in a state of despair with low expectations like a victim of their own impairment instead of taking on a challenge to better themselves. There are also some stereotypes where they are portrayed as a hero as well but there in that situation they overcome their disability. Examples like a paralysed man learning to walk again and the challenges they need to overcome from living with their impairment. In some fantasy dramas like comic book action heroes the disability is shown as a superpower like ability. Consider the Daredevil, a Marvel comic book character whose real identity is Matt Murdoch. Murdoch is a blind lawyer whose impairment has been caused by a chemical accident that caused his other senses to function with super sharp abilities. Through this he acts as a crime fighter working as a lawyer by day and a vigilante at night.

 While there are few heroes and more victims there are also a lot of villains with disabilities as well, specifically mental health which is often presented as a motivation for the perpetrator of the story. This type of character is driven to commit crime or revenge for resentment of their disability. A lot of villains in TV shows and films portray this trait hence why they are stereotypically 'mad hate filled psychopaths'. It is a negative and cruel perception that doesn't really bear anything in real life. Leading psychiatrists have proved that most violent crimes are not linked to mental illnesses. But there are some characters who have a positive use of their mental health like CIA agent Carrie Mathison in Homeland who has bipolar disorder. She uses her disability in a positive and constructive manner by playing to the strengths that her disability gives her. That includes an obsessive attachment to the case that she is assigned and going above and beyond to achieve her goals. Although Carrie does have manic episodes and relies on medication she doesn't appear as an insufferable protagonist. In some cases her disability makes her mind sharper.

I wanted an autistic character who was a hero that would show his own strength in the real world, to prove that through all the challenges that life throws at him, he doesn't necessarily need to overcome the limitations of his mental health, instead he shows the best qualities that come from within. That was an interesting experiment in breaking away from stereotypes of mental health. But at the same time it also allowed me to explore the divisions and injustice that was hidden beneath the agenda of civil rights and equality campaigners.

Let me start with a story about a recent act of fighting for freedom in which I was a prominent and vocal activist that involved speaking up for a group that consisted of all classes of citizens that was made up of people from all walks of life. Including mental health, race, national identity in a struggle for freedom that unravelled the hidden agenda which saw prejudice on a scale that hadn't been unlike anything in recent years. That was the Referendum on the European Union. A referendum that uncovered a brave new world.

When I was fighting the campaign on the Leave side I was engaged in a battle of wills against Remain. Both sides fought with a focus on certain issues that would play a central part in the campaign. Remain focused on preserving the union to keep the economy intact, while Leave focused on immigration that was a problem for many ordinary citizens who felt that they were being dismissed and vilified by the liberal metropolitan elite to protect the hierarchy that kept them in their place. That vilification had been around for a very long time and was used in propaganda from both sides. As I was on Leave's team I had to put up with some accusations of xenophobia, racism, berating from the elite and treated as deplorables. They also accused us of being economically illiterate and lacking in ambition to consider that freeing ourselves from the EU would not only allow us to decide on how we forge ahead with our destiny but that we would be a second-class nation of no significance. That statement reminded me of the way that I am patronised and stigmatised because of my autistic spectrum disorder, in which case they thought of me as a vulnerable and inferior creature who is a sub species of class that is not worth saving. From my point of view the Remain activists were like overlords seeking to substitute the working classes through a continued process of social engineering in which we ought to be replaced with a foreign class of cheap labour. The Remain and Leave sides fought each other like an old fashioned peasants revolt with Remain trying to tempt voters with happiness at the expense of their freedom.

At the time of writing this I had just read 'Brave New World' written in 1932 by Aldous Huxley. This novel has been compared to George Orwell's 'Nineteen Eighty-Four' and both novels tell of a dystopian future of oppression. Orwell's vision was based on a brutal thought controlling totalitarian state using pain to subvert the will of the masses. Huxley's novel uses oppression and enslavement through pleasure and happiness where the masses are made to accept the pleasures of everyday life to make the economy rich with no individual thinking for wealth creation. Whereas Orwell's vision has become a prophecy that liberal campaigners use to protect freedom Huxley's vision has become forgotten in the midst of wealth creation and prosperity. In the case of the EU campaign Huxley's anti-utopia is reflected in the standards of the liberal elite who have created so much liberalism and tolerance that condemns anything that disagrees with it's thinking as xenophobia and counter productivity.

Well democracy works by being accountable to it's actions, the EU with it's anti-democratic laws work in favour of the higher classes so that they can protect the industries and services that work in their favour. I was campaigning for Leave on a basis of promoting hopeful, creative economic development and innovation. I am a science geek and I wanted to unleash a catalogue of great ideas and policies that make Britain prosperous. I didn't have any qualms with immigrants, if anything I was fed up with being made to feel ashamed of my standing in society by a governing body of people who felt that certain industries and communities were expendable. The real taboo wasn't a race issue it was class shaming. A shaming of a person's class might not be so much of a race issue but it is equally offensive. In January 2017 a radio caller called Alex who claimed to be an ex-working class man told LBC radio station how much he wanted to "teach the working class a lesson" in a patronising rant. Alex fumed about how working class people moan about their situation claiming that they "don't fight for betterness from an employer or educate themselves to get out their situation" and ignoring how rich the UK has become under the EU. I once wrote on my blog about how this situation amounted to a Huxley Indictment. In 'Brave New World' babies are conditioned to avoid certain things like books and natural objects so that they don't appreciate the right things that are needed to allow for creativity, imagination, innovation and aspiration. In the same way the people of many western countries are made to think like that. The system that made Alex the way he thinks explains why the working classes of this country don't educate themselves enough, they have been made to think of themselves as a class who are insignificant next to their betters who govern them. Hence why they generally are apathetic to political and social issues. These progressive liberals think that elevating people's standing in society is more important than recognising the creative potential and usefulness of these people with objectivism. It is a way of life described by Ayn Rand in her novel 'Atlas Shrugged', in which people's intelligence are stunted and their use of imagination is impotent. This has led to a dystopia where the ruling elite have crushed the common man to a state of oppression and is refused a means of advancement.

Alex has clearly no regards to the backbone of his society and doesn't recognise the importance of the working classes. Before he elevated himself into a high class what he didn't appreciate was that these are the people responsible for growing our food, repairing our utility machinery, running the fuel supplies and public transport needed to make the wheels of the economy and the country work in motion so that we can go to work and play well. Try and show appreciation and understand their significance to your life before you start berating them for their standing in society. Betterness is available to anyone to suit their individual needs whatever their situation and we need to show them how much we appreciate them.

And that is something that I think is the real problem in tackling inequality, we are shaming people for thinking prejudiced thoughts not to different races but certain races that are favoured by ethnicity or class rather than difference. That's why I as a mental health person struggle with being accepted by other races and religions who think that the class that I am a part of is a taboo that should not be seen or heard.

Race and religion is a subject that isn't often explored in issues with mental health and disablement. But I believe that they are closely connected to each other because they are all under the same umbrella that entails the mission of the civil rights movement. In the history of the civil rights movement the fight for equality has been very slow to progress and to eliminate prejudice towards ethnic groups, disablement, religions and genders. However, in the fight for equality and social justice there is always a question of who needs it most. But when we decide who needs it most who or what group is most deserving and what is it based on? The less able and vulnerable like the disabled? The most conscious religious groups like Christians? The most persecuted and vilified religious groups like the Muslims? The wealthiest minority groups who are so rich and powerful like the Jews? The most intelligent and gifted who are capable of making science and art fulfilling like autism? The backbone of British society which is made up of common folk like the working classes?

You rarely hear people of mental health talk about race, religion and nationality. Out of all these groups mental health is considered to be the most stigmatised and they are often seen as the forgotten group within the Civil Rights movement. In the years that I have been an activist I have found myself within a group that hasn't actually been fighting for equality but fighting for my own share of rights and liberties. Over the last 50 years, civil rights groups have found themselves short changed by one another to get their own share of laws to protect them. During the Civil Rights Movement of the 1950-60s the number of new laws that were enacted by the government were based primarily for the acceptance of blacks into society. This was largely in part to the fact that they accounted for the majority of those who were suffering from segregation and lacking in social mobility.

Martin Luther King's vision of the way people thought about race marked the start of a social revolution for building a peaceful nation of love and justice between fellow human beings. He dedicated his life to this cause and in doing so I think he may have thought of that dream towards mental health as well. In his famous 'I Have a Dream' speech he quoted one of the statements in the US Declaration of Independence written by Thomas Jefferson that 'We hold these truths to be self-evident: that all men are created equal'. That quotation written in 1776 has been paraphrased by many other constitutions and activists across the world over the last three hundred years. There is some contradiction in that speech that I find incredible. In the case of a disabled person the creator has made the person unequal in appearance or mentality. As a mental health person on the autistic spectrum I have been made incapable of one ability or more but I and many others like me have been blessed with an amazing ability to light up the world in a way that makes us worthy of acceptance that entitles us to the rights of life, liberty and the pursuit of happiness. The paragraph that contains that phrase 'All men are created equal' also states 'that they are endowed by their Creator with certain unalienable Rights'. This applies to all human beings abled or disabled and therefore all human beings equal or unequal in nature deserve the same rights. Later in the 20th century new equality laws where emphasis was put on recognising disabled people as part of their constitutions ensured that even those that were created unequal rightly deserved the same treatment. Thus their condition is not a taboo subject and can be talked about as being normal.

Martin Luther King also had in that dream to see that one day that his children and all people would be judged differently as well. Although people on the autistic spectrum are not judgemental characters they do struggle to accept things that are not alike them because they struggle to adapt to change. I read on an internet forum called Wrong Planet about an Aspergic person who came from a family of British National Party supporters. The BNP is a far-right British political party that is no longer operating, but it used to be famous for some of it's extreme views on multiculturalism. The man put forward a question that his mental health condition may have made him racist as he felt uncomfortable living around non-white people and he had only just recently been diagnosed with the condition. None of which is true, mental health people are not inherently or naturally racist. It's just that they are psychologically fearful of change and situations that are unfamiliar with them. They keep in routines that make them comfortable with their surroundings. In some cases, the slightest disruption in their routine can make them terrified or disturbed. I have had my own moments with being disturbed by changes in my social situations like being surrounded by other ethnic groups but not in a way that would make me feel vengeful and hurtful towards them. I embrace all classes of citizens based on the best qualities of that person and that group for all the honour and glory that they bring to the civilised world in the name of freedom and justice.

The last paragraph of 'I Have a Dream' speech contains a paragraph that speaks of allowing freedom to ring for all groups of people on God's Green Earth. I too dream of a nation where people are able to practice their freedoms regardless of their group but it's a difficult struggle for freedom to prevail when the government only approves of one type of group to express themselves freely without bias against another group. Be it black or white, Christian or Muslim or Jew or Sikh or Hindu, British or European, able or disabled, etc.

Although many establishment figures and white people had contempt and opposition for the Civil Rights Movement there was also opposition to civil rights from people within the Movement itself. The majority of the Movement was made up of blacks followed by woman, other religious groups, other ethnic groups, homosexuals, the disabled, mental health, etc. When the Civil Rights Movement began it was supposed to have fought for equality based on universality of each other, but later the Movement splinted as the groups started to realise that they were getting less than the majority of the groups within the Movement and that their own issues were not being heeded. This is one of the main reasons why fighting for equality is such a slow and difficult process. Although all people should be treated equal some people consider their group to be more equal than others. This is the issue that mental health has concerns for in regards to equality and civil rights.

The acceptance of mental health and the disabled into the mainstream has by far been the longest of the equality battles to fight for it's own rights. If you take a look at the equality campaigns over the last 60 years you'll find that they have only come to favour certain groups at different times. First the Black and Asian community won their rights in the 1960s, then woman got their own rights in the 1970s to eliminate prejudice between genders, then the gay and lesbian community got their share of rights in the 1980s, and then finally disablement got their own discrimination laws in the 1990s followed in the 2000s by social experiments to unite all the diverse groups together in a way which resulted in multiculturalism. Unfortunately this was an experiment that resulted in disharmony and dogma. Now there appears to be a fight for a share of the rights and liberties of each of these groups to balance the equality laws in their favour. I should know because I have been educated in an all-inclusive community school where I shared classes with all types of races, religions, ethnic and social groups.

My school was in a deprived area of Bethnal Green which at that point in time had a large migrant community mostly made up of Bangladeshi origin Asians and there was a lot of socially disadvantaged families. Later I discovered the school's bad performance was also reflected in it's Ofsted Report. I saw a lot of bullying and banter between each ethnic group because of their differences to one another. I saw blacks and whites picking on each other, Hindus and Sikhs keeping their distance from each other, black African kids getting into fights with black Asian kids. The school staff didn't pay much attention to this social crisis that was going on but it was so noisy and awful I couldn't stand to be in there. As an autistic person it just wasn't right for me because I didn't cope very well and I was prone to having mental fits of anger and breakdowns. Some of these pupils saw me as a target to take advantage of my vulnerability for fun. There were some other disabled pupils in the school with me who were often excluded from some of the activities taking place there. It didn't even matter if they were badly behaved because there were no failing grades here. What I hated the most was being made to take responsibility for other people's problems here. Despite being in denial about my mental health at the time I wasn't granted any disability management programme or mental health practitioners. All I had for support were study support workers who just sat beside me in the classroom and insisted that I carry on with my studying like a cow being prepared for the cattle market. This school showed an example of what happens when equality laws are disorganised. I would say that I went to a school in a segregated area of London. This is not good for a country that is supposed to embrace diversity when the ethnic groups it supports think of themselves as being more significant than the other class, race or ethnic group they co-exist with.

The topic of ethnic groups and mental health is a controversial one and when a mental health person is put in this situation it can be volatile. Mental health with race and religion exposes a double dose of prejudice and we are afraid to speak out about it because it results in a time bomb that explodes with unimaginable chaos. Some people from non-white backgrounds have got mental health issues themselves and they experience dual-discrimination both for their race and their mental issues. Earlier I showed that when rights are granted to ethnic groups we often allow them to practice parts of the culture that clash with the rights and liberties of other groups and the civil rights enshrined in the laws of the country. Consider the Bangladeshi culture that I was at school with. According to a report from the World Bank about the attitudes to disablement (including mental health conditions) in Bangladesh, disabled people often suffer discrimination and are excluded from society and don't have access to basic services. In a country that is a member of the World Health Organisation and has little pro-disability legislations the disabled are seen as 'fearful and superstitious beings'. Many people in Bangladesh see disabled people as a curse or a cause of embarrassment for a family and there is little sympathy to the situation of these people with disabilities.

When we criticise one group of people because of their cultural beliefs or their crimes against innocent people we find ourselves judging them in their favour for the protection of their rights and liberties. This is where race and mental health issues require an intervention for their protection by the law and the state. It questions whether we are granting one group with more rights than the other that have a special privilege to be excused disciplining for attacking another group. This is something that has resulted in accusations of racism every time there is criticism towards these actions. But it's not a case of racism it's just plain culture shaming. Shaming a group to show that you are protecting another group's rights and liberties. But what exactly are you protecting in the name of civil rights and liberties when you are allowing mental health to suffer?

In January 2017 a group of four African Americans attacked a mentally ill white man in Chicago in a horrific assault that was streamed live on Facebook. The victim had been an easy target because of his vulnerability and the black gang who attacked him lured him to an apartment block where the attack took place. It went on for five hours where he was slashed, slapped in several places, bound, gagged, punched and had his head stomped in. The attack stopped when the attackers were disturbed and the victim ran off to get help from a police officer in the street.

In the video his attackers were yelling obscenities at home saying 'Fuck Donald Trump' and 'Fuck White People'. It's not known if he was a voter of Donald Trump but the attackers probably had a motive to make it out of their hatred of white people and their dismay for Trump becoming president of the United States. The attack was treated by the Chicago Police as a hate crime, but not a race crime, even though it was there in the video for all the world to see. The general consensus is that in order for the protection of diversity and race relations in the community, criticisms of minorities should not be allowed. Well in the context of this the mental health community is less significant than the black community in vulnerability and standing in society. Some news reporters even supported that it wasn't a race crime neither and some black rights campaigners even condemned the attackers for shaming the black community. But I am not concerned about the race issue with this attack, I am much more interested in how the leftist-liberal agenda permits certain groups to have double standards in life. That's not equality that is a case for ethnic nationalism. A form of nationalism that states that people of certain ethnic origin should be allowed to practice what is part of their culture even if it goes against the decent civilised nature of the society that nation supports.

If you continue to dismiss the way this crime is a race hate thing then you are building a case to support segregation and apartheid, as if you would rather not integrate and promote diversity. In which case it seems that races and mental health people should be kept apart from one another. But that's not the kind of society that we would want to live in. It's a far cry from the type of society that Nelson Mandela fought for. This civil rights campaigner fought to eliminate apartheid from South Africa and did it out of love and civil justice between fellow human beings and so that the black population could live in mutual harmony with the white population.

When he ruled South Africa he didn't wish any grudge upon the white people and certainly didn't approve of the vengeful acts of violence that followed upon his release from prison. As Mandela didn't want neither black or white domination neither do I want any domination by able bodied or disabled bodied.

 What good nature makes mental health worthy of rights and liberties? Well despite their mental difficulties they do have great talents to share with people with the way their minds work. But that talent is being dismissed because it is either being ignored or being made to feel ashamed of what people may think of them because of their mental health. In the years that I have lived in a multi-cultural Britain I have found that most of the cultures find mental health to be the least equal of all groups defined by civil and social activists. This is one of the reasons why I as a mental health person sympathize with people who have support right wing politics like nationalism. Nationalism is long considered to be an enemy of diversity because it puts the country first at the expense of minorities making it look racist, xenophobic and alienating communities. But they are wrong.

Let's look at a way in which we can settle this social injustice so that we can be free to live on good terms. Nationalism in itself can take on many different forms: white, black, left wing, right wing, cultural, ethnic, civic, neo, etc. All of which have a shared communal identification based on the core values of identity, self-determination and solidarity. Nationalism is good for righting the injustice and discontent that is tearing the different social groups apart. It grants a sense of belonging to allow liberties and rights to exist so that all human beings can live together in a civilised way. Which is unusual when liberal leftists say that nationalism stokes up tension and division between communities, yet they promote a form of nationalism that rejects their own views. This is my attempt to reason the case for civic and cultural nationalism that is fit for all classes and types of people to agree to.

Civic nationalism is a non-xenophobic form of nationalism compatible with values of freedom, tolerance, equality and individual rights. It is about creating a place where people of all countries, creeds, races, religions and mental health can come together at the table to discuss and create a country with a mutual bond between each other. With civic nationalism we defend the value of national identity because people need it to lead meaningful, autonomous lives. Civic nationalism teaches that polities need national identity to function properly and to avoid a pestilential division of complacency and prejudice between it's people. This type of nationalism lies within traditions of rationalism and liberalism and it is practiced by many Western democracies. By comparison Eastern nations use a type of nationalism based on ethnicity. In these nations ethnic nationalism is defined by a shared heritage which includes a number of common things: language, religion and ethnic ancestry. It's also includes ideas of a culture shared by members of the group that makes up the majority of the population. If you think that nationalism is the countermeasure to diversity then you are wrong, it builds the solid foundation that is needed to protect diversity laws including those of mental health. Ethnic nationalism upholds and approves the culture and faith, while civic nationalism protects the freedom and equality for all classes of citizens.

There's also another form of nationalism that can be intertwined with civic nationalism that represents a shared culture that focuses on national identity shaped by cultural traditions and language. This is called cultural nationalism. It's a broad church type nationalism that means it accepts a broad range of different forms of nationalism that is not independent of other ideologies. So it works for both civic and ethnic nationalism. It encompasses a feeling of cultural pride so that it puts the fabric of society stitched together in a way that is acceptable to all types of people so that all races, religions and abilities can live in the same space. It's ethnically diverse in people with common cultural beliefs and diversity, but not common race or ancestry. This is shown in the ideas and feelings of cultural nationalism are built upon shared cultural ideals and norms among a society. This includes different ideologies practiced by the differently elected democratic parties, national holidays, shared cuisine, etc. What's also great about this way of celebrating national culture is that it relies on integration of different groups so that they share their lives without fighting for different things to shunt themselves away from each other. In the case of British culture, we bring together all groups of people that allows mental health, disablement, religion, nationalities and races to integrate and ingratiate ourselves in the spirit of the nation.

 By accepting mental health into the mainstream is can also help solve a social problem like terrorism and segregation. In this war on terrorism by religious fanatics, mental health can be a recognised means of curing us of this warped perverted version of Islam that thrives in isolated communities. I would like to share my abilities with religious leaders as well. These radicals who attack people with bombs and machetes are mentally unstable. Although many psychiatrists believe that mental health is not a cause of hatred that motivates them to kill the practice of mental health can be used to cure their poisonous thoughts. Terrorists are radicalised using the techniques that is also applied to mentally vulnerable people by brainwashing. If you replace the negative thoughts of this propaganda with positive thoughts, then you can make them show off the best qualities of their religion without wishing death on innocent people. I can prove this for myself because when I was young I lived a semi-segregated existence with negative thinking that kept me from bettering myself. But when I broke this dogmatic point of view I realised that my mental health and abilities could make something good out of me. So if you can embrace mental health in society then you can beat terrorism and stop this warped perversion of a peaceful religion from causing havoc and destruction upon people. By bringing out the 'best qualities' of a peaceful religion like Islam and combine it with the mental health community you can create a country where all classes of citizens can live in harmony. I want to see that harmony occur but it can't happen when you reject the challenge for integration. I know that out of this inequality must come something good. All you need to do is come forth and share it with the world, just like what I do with my autism.

In 2014 I was a volunteer at the Commonwealth Games in Glasgow where I befriended a woman on social media after I gave her hope in a response to a post where she said: I feel that having a disability and daring to ask for 'help' is a dirty word, I feel like a second class citizen. My response was: Don't think like that, I am autistic - Aspergers to be precise. To ask for help like that gives us the means to adjust to the world around us. Believe me, no one is a second class citizen. For me all forms of life are unequal, we should tolerate and accept all classes of citizens.

Equality campaigners and activists for race and religion should take heed from activists for mental health. For they are the missing piece of the puzzle to bring freedom and justice to the lives of everyone.

CHAPTER EIGHT

For Scott to be concerned nothing in life mattered for himself. If it did then it would mean locking himself in isolation rather than going out to prove himself. But despite his efforts he was always in the wrong place at the wrong time like a new book on the wrong shelf. But he hadn't been out in the open for such a long time. *As I spent most of my time in isolation, I learnt a great deal about what was going on from the outside world. All that time on the internet reading and digesting on information that's led me to become a journalist. I'm surprised hardly anyone takes it seriously to have their voice to it. The sad bastards!* He didn't like the way many people took it as 'coffee break gossip'. Even his confrontation with lawyer Jane Glouster was an influence he hadn't tried before. It wasn't that he was gutless; it was due to lack of experience and opportunity.

Having seen the death of Tariq and learnt of the cause of the explosion, Scott felt that no real law could protect him or anyone else. *Too obsessed with their privileges to bother about reality, I think.* There was more oppression and injustice for disablement than there is for ethnic minorities. He could only undo his own problems with society. Stepping over to the crooked brief Scott wished she'd died from her wounds. *Then that way I wouldn't have to battle with her.* But what about a possibility that it might be worth giving the satisfaction of saving her. *Maybe... Just maybe... I can prove myself right to everyone the poison of justice is poisoned by their own architects.*

After a quick peek at Jane, Scott made his way back to the second carriage. Gliding over the gap between the two carriages he noticed a couple of rats were trying to climb up between the gap. 'As with the Underground you've got countless things associated with the dark and gloomy. Rats, cobwebs, dust, soot. I wonder if it's anything like a horror film?' Scott's whispering thoughts were from his playful past he had with Hornby Railways. He used to live next to a railway junction, admiring the action of the train depot from his window. Sometimes he would watch the action and imagine adventures in the depot taking place there. Playing train games in the house, watching repeats of Thomas the Tank Engine. This life's adventure had given him experience to deal with the Underground.

Nick had moved up onto the seats. In the minutes after the small fires had been extinguished somehow. From a best guess, the soot from the tunnels must have had sand extracts in them, extinguishing the flames as it hurtled into the rancid tunnel following the explosion. Nick glanced down at the bandage Scott had given him earlier. He sneaked a peek at his flesh gash for the extent of the damage. Gutted and shocked he ties it back up to forget as he can.

Scott called out dashing back to Nick. 'Are you okay?' Scott started going funny. It was almost as if he was going to be sick. As he struggled over to Nick, Scott felt the full force of a fit coming up his spine. He was rapidly blinking and could feel involuntarily spasms of his facial muscles. *Oh bloody hell! Here it comes again. The odd occasional grimace brought on by motor clumsiness. Namely a nervous shiver running down my spine.* Moving about he looked like a wooden performer with a puppet motive. Scott gradually went into a trance. Breathing in and out into his palms with twenty breaths to relax himself. When he relieved the instability he was back to normal. A thing like this wasn't always humiliating. Up until a few years ago he managed to use it by exhaling stress and anxiety.

Gathering strength, he moved towards Nick who looked nauseated. Scott didn't want to slap more injuries on him, but if he had to in order to bring him round, then there was no problem. At first Scott was a bit worried he had forgotten the man's name. 'Excuse me, are you alright?' Like an obsessive compulsive sufferer, he was worried about what he might have forgotten. But with a mind burnt with details and facts of events there was nothing wrong with taking snap guesses. 'Nick!' Scott slightly shook the man to affiliate with him.

'What, what is it?' Nick's voice was muffled by his state of mind.

'For a moment I thought you were gone then.' said Scott. 'Do you remember me from the last time?'

'Yes, that's right.' Nick tried not to trip up on his memory. 'Is it Peter?'

'It's Scott!' he retorted. Disturbed by his own mind he jiggered sideways adjacent to Nick. Nick adamant that his condition was driving Scott crazy, knew very little about an autistic person's way of life. Scott had to keep his calm and composure which he was trying to do, and having seen what the motive of the bomber had, he needed to avoid negative thoughts to avoiding exploding into a meltdown if not an explosion of nerves. Nick depended on Scott to get him out of here and Scott needed to let the world know that he was able enough to do it.

'Scott, what about what you told me earlier.' said Nick. 'About your problem, disability or whatever. Well are you still up for that? Can you still get by with it?'

'Yes. Yes, I'm alright.' he spoke weakly. 'I'm just going through a retarded period that's all.'

'What do you mean by retarded?' asked Nick. The idea of disabled person calling himself a retard sounded self-degrading. But it wasn't like that.

'Well I guess that's just the way I like to call it.' said Scott. 'I am okay with the use of so called derogatory terms about my autism spectrum disorder. Not all disabled people with happy with the effects of their impairments. I've learnt to adapt to them so that I don't have to get so angry.'

'Sounds like you don't care for that politically correct attitude to diversity.'

'Correct. I can't stand it, it's like thought control. That's not right, it affects a person's imagination and intelligence. No two brains think alike and I am not prone to sensitivity thanks to boxing. Providing that cocky lawyer isn't so bloody strict!'

'Lawyer, what lawyer?' asked Nick.

'Yes, back there in the carriage up front where the big bang is.' Now motivated by his own disability, Scott felt shallow like he'd just come up a beach towards his enemies. 'I just came across a human rights lawyer who made a mental health person miserable. An enemy of democracy. A fascist liberal.' Scott explained what he had learnt to Nick and what the case was about. How Glouster had inflicted more misery on a disabled person making him out to be an illogical and pointless case worth fighting for. As if the only freedom to protect is for those with too much money and no accountability. 'People like her think that if nothing is that Craine's fault then it's not his company that is at fault that they fired him.'

'But that means you've also got a got a chance at getting a payout for this. Surely that lawyer would act as a spokesperson.' As Nick gestured at the damaged train, Scott could see the obvious. But the way he took a literal interpretation of things Scott was not taking on this one. He had another idea in mind. *A compensation claim is just about bribery. Bribery to yourself, digging out the past into your own guilt. Burying the past is all about justice.*

'Maybe, but I loathe the people like her. I am sick of pathetic patronising social justice warriors. There always there to get in the way of the real victims. As far as they are concerned, our problems exist for them to make money. They are instrumental in a society that teaches that no one has any responsibility for themselves, there is money for nothing and you are blinded by the spoils of your own society.'

Nick thought for a moment about what Scott was expressing to him. He could see that Scott had a point to prove positive. 'So what you saying is that this person is not to be trusted and that she is corrupt.'

'Correct, you expect us to entrust our injuries to a profiteer!' Protested Scott. 'That is like creating a problem for the sake of others to suffer so that you can get rich.'

'That's right.' Said Nick. I've read about it a few times in the papers. The sights they make of lags walking free from courts and magistrates. Most or some of these laws make money for the law firms and corporations.'

'The thought of another immorally bankrupt narcissist winning again would be unbearable.' said Scott cautiously. 'Even if she did any good her past in supporting criminals is a reflection of her character. Never compensation, the real problem is getting justice that is deserved.' *And as for my own sake, I hope I get an opportunity and a right to prove positive for autism today, before I unleash my strength against her. Fiddling the law to turn justice into a joke.*

Scott turned his eyes towards the front carriage. Scott went back curious to see the better of her once more. This time like he was diving into a war zone. Always hyperactively motivated when he was on fire. Noticing a scene up front he cooled down to tackle the problem. A tackle that might put the true nature of this horrendous humanitarian crime rightfully in the dock.

CHAPTER NINE

Jane took second minute glances at the victims noting their liability to vengeance by their injuries. 'Punishment by revenge is not right, it's just not what you need right now.' she said to a victim. 'I'll see to it that you get your say on the matter.' She played it as a game inventing the rules as she went along promising lavish handouts and asserting her own liberal agenda. To her rights of liberty were all about protecting people's rights to a collective interest for the establishment's end and for that there must be no prejudice thoughts. If a victim wanted to see justice done that didn't matter, the only thing that she gave a care for was that she could undo the conflict by collective jurisdiction in a public inquiry.

As a means of greed with Jane, she just didn't see the crisis as a conflict of victims and terrorists. Through her eyes it was a personnel opportunity.

Politicians and immoral bankrupt stateswoman are weaknesses that just should stay away from each other. That revolting witch is just plain blind, stupid and callous for all there is to see. They call me a retard for being mentally unstable, well in normal land you can find people who are ten times a retard like the people of my kind. Back in school Scott was very sympathetic towards the other kid's social outcomes. Victims of oppression and cheaters let loose by bureaucracy that treated others like dogs. He had a friend who was bullied just as much as he did but it was ignored by the school governors who were more interested in protecting their reputation to get the school good reports. Instead of removing the bully, they removed him to avoid the embarrassment of seeing a minority being intimidated and moved school. Despite trying to blend in with society there were mostly mindless reactions for his efforts. Getting punched for being different. He was like a socialist outcast wrongly placed in a battlefield. Just like most autistics suffer from. Even now with a member of the law, who knew nothing of injustice except for those they cherry pick to deserve the rights over another class, he felt like he had to crush a bad apple.

At the driver's cab a man was hammering on the door. Earlier after the explosion he'd just been talking to the driver, trying to get him to open the door to the cab. He had been trying to look through where the peephole was now replaced with a punch hole. He couldn't make out what had happened to the driver upfront. Instincts told him the driver was lying unconscious on the floor to the cab. 'Hold on I'm going to get you out of there.' He scuttled around to look for some kind of wrench. The butt end of a seat handle was the first useful thing he found. He turned it on the door frame, where the complications ensued the door opens towards him. So he protruded the implement on the edge of the door.

'Who are you supposed to be then?' butted in Jane.

'I'm Paul and I'm getting out of here.' said Paul. 'Can't you see?'

Jane countermanded like a pointless juvenile. 'What do you think you're doing there? That's out of bounds to people like you.'

'Yes well, we need to get out of here.' Said an exasperated Paul.

'Never mind that.' said Jane. 'Besides the driver should be in there anyway.'

'Well that's the point because in there right now the driver is badly hurt and I need to get to him.'

'So you can get to him when the emergency services get here.' stated Jane. 'Own you own problems.'

'So I just forget about him cause he's gonna die at any minute, is that what you're saying?' retorted Paul.

'Maybe he might have to die, that way at least you won't have to bother. But these other people might survive though, I know better so sit down. Having sympathy for people who kill people is bad enough. I tried to get me you know.'

'How so?' insisted Paul. 'He tried to kill me you know. don't see why your live is more important than the rest of us.'

'Maybe, but I'm in a higher authority here. So if the security service failed then you should listen more wisely.' said Jane. 'I can make something that will make things all the better.' Then Jane looked up and thought about Craine's cry for help. 'For God sake I wish he had just topped himself in private. If he was mentally ill, then he shouldn't have been so selfish and taken other people with him.'

'Why do you keep talking about your own ego?' Said Paul. 'Your acting like that guy did something to you that didn't deserve to happen and that it's all about you. And that's very hurtful about a mentally ill person. You should be sticking up for people with problems like that otherwise they become a timebomb.'

'Because she's a politically motivated moron, that's why.' said Scott. As he raged in from the back, he gritted his teeth.

'Be quiet.' insisted Jane. 'I can see that you have a problem with getting involved with this so make sure you're alright and I'll see to it that you are okay. I think as a person with Aspergers you don't realise how vulnerable you are...'

'Don't do that!' insisted Scott. 'Now listen to me, now all disabled people are happy with the circumstances of their impairments. You are talking to me like I'm a stupid brainless vegetable. I am sick of it and I will not have my battles fought for by a malicious witch for the likes of you! You know nothing!'

'What use are you?' asked Jane. 'Just an attention seeking twat. Are the benefits not good enough for you?'

'I think your briefcase has got nothing but propaganda to promote pleasure to make people ignore the reality.' Said Scott. 'Why would I even want welfare handouts, I love the freedom to protect liberties, not liberties to allow people to be stupid and reckless like a Trotskyite supremacist.'

'Don't talk to me about supremacism, remember your condition!' Said Jane. 'You are mentally ill and vulnerable and shouldn't try to be better than other people. You'll just make yourself completely insufferable.'

'So now human rights outlaw what they're supposed to be in favour: freedom of speech. Is that right?' stated Scott. 'I would've thought they'd be turning against the law abiding public for a long time. Tell me what makes you think that it's a human right for a boss to dismiss a mental health person using that charter of bureaucracy to suit your own agenda?'

'Article 11, paragraph 1: The right to freedom of assembly and to freedom of association of others. That is to protect the company and the boss from dangerous people who are likely to be liable to make them capable of committing a crime. He was mentally unstable and could be likely to cause a dangerous accident lead on by his mental illness.' She acted in a posh toff manner, as if she held his card for crunching.

'That's just it? Is that how much you value disablement? Slaves to obsolescence and oppression. Cabbages to be rocked along rickety old social-liberalist vegetable stalls crying out for sympathy and asking for donations? That is just pure ableism. Stupidly manipulating and fiddling your own professional conduct?'

'I'm not, I'm protecting you lot from further harm to other people, in turn it's showing that it's possible to prevent further harm to others.' Jane then added. 'Why should a mentally ill person even be allowed to advance themselves. Fair enough I can understand some of them are able, but considering that people like Craine has no chance of being accepted into work anymore he should forget his aspirations. You are just defective and hopeless. Try considering those who are unable to wash and feed themselves.'

'Oh really, you expect me to conform to a set standards of idleness and consider you a hero when you're a crook.' said Scott without an angry tone, as his prosody could not project his verbal feelings properly. 'Do you understand me? They are dead. I might not be able to empathise with people but I know right from wrong and in some respects I'm much more intelligent than you without the need to be a cold condescending supremacist.' He pointed to where the fanatic had left a crater. 'The name of a good citizen turned into a madman, shamed by stigma and that was brought on by the people of your kind who infantilise people's perception of mental health.'

'Infantilise!' Said Jane. 'I have made people aware of how special you are and what makes them worth saving for.'

'The problem is not your awareness campaign it's what rights we have. According to you disablement is about being vulnerable and defeated and that we should not advance their abilities.' Said Scott. 'In effect you are pushing legislation to enslave them through pleasurable activities. It's a Huxley indictment.'

'A what indictment?' asked Jane.

'Aldous Huxley, writer of a Brave New World.' Said Scott. 'It's a futuristic novel about a society that uses drugs and propaganda in the form of pleasure and happiness to make you blind about reality. Well I realised years ago that all those endless drugs and charity campaigns that make being depressed something to be amused by. To end the stigma of mental health you don't make it cool to be a cripple or crazy, you embrace the diverse nature of a mental health person's best qualities.'

Scott's emotional discontent could not relate himself in any way to the bomber's motives or feelings. An ability useful enough in repelling the dark and disturbing thoughts he had that the crooked lawyer would use against him. Aspergers made him non-judgemental but he had a drive to make a stand against this liberal immoral carcass who think's people should not think prejudice thoughts. *I maybe low on the communication/relationship department but I can never let that be used against me. All I know I know is what is right and what needs to be undone by what that crooked woman did to turn it on us. Offering all those filthy scum's free tickets out of jail and making money out of the chaos. I 'am proud to be compassionate so for the sake of God, have judicial pride without political prejudice.*

'Those fanatics in power love causing trouble.' said Scott. 'They act like death and destruction is inevitable and that we should embrace the chaos. Shame on you, you're a selfish condescending witch who think I should be kept in place. The real evil in this world is those who can't stand people who don't think alike them. So don't lecture me on hate.'

'Alright if that's what you believe then that's fine, but don't think anyone will listen to you for an opinion.' Jane could only look up to him as a sick victim of society. With a good training programme to brainwash him from the negative thoughts that make the real thing. But Scott's point of view revealed her true colours and above all where her true backstabbing loyalties lie. 'Maybe you can believe it but if there is a public hearing then you will probably find yourself vilifying mental health.'

Scott had a sinking feeling. As he walked up to Jane, his anxiety trembled with chronic determination. 'You know what...you are nothing but lost in your own little world. Mental health in the capacity of a villain like you is treated as an instrument of destruction. Look around you...there is only a place for human rights and they are for decent people. The human rights laws were brought into force to prevent the atrocities of inhuman degradation. You are using a double think method on human rights. Only a civil rights act can set people's hatred aside. I want to be able to integrate with society and to do that is to get people to accept the best qualities of their differences and share the land to establish a land of hope and glory.'

'You're wrong.' yelped Jane. 'Disablement in the working world or even contributing to a society is a waste of time. You in your mental condition can't fulfil anything and you don't understand people. That's why they are only worth protecting for, besides in business my friends say that weak people are a waste of space. From what you are saying to me I believe they should not and cannot trust themselves to make a decision. Besides sometimes they have conflicts with certain ethnic groups that lead to prejudice with race.'

'Well that doesn't surprise me.' Said Scott. 'I've seen every social justice warrior suffer in their fight for freedom. It's all because of a conflict of cultures where instead of embracing a common interest that brings peace and harmony they just fight for a special right of liberty for them to crush and vilify their opponents. That's why we are sleep walking into segregation and becoming strangers to each other.' Then Scott started to become really agitated and stared into her face. 'And while we are on the subject, you would probably start playing the race issue. Well if you can silence people with social liberal supremacy language then you might want to consider the ism that you are using on me – ableism. Fucking ableist is all you are.'

'Swearing at me isn't any help.' Jane was senseless and stubborn, as Scott was trying to prove a point. While she was resisting his thinking, she just thought about running away and ignoring him. 'Now you're starting to harass me.'

'I've given up taking people's things literally years ago, thanks to social skills classes I can spot when a person is trying to undermine me, liberal scum.'

Jane continued to anti-protest. 'I think you are starting to become just like a terrorist as well, I really do feel sorry for you. Your really doing the disabled community a disservice.'

'So to sum it all in common sense - which you'd rather politically correct - you'd rather I'd submit to the state services and assume that you are right about everything to do with autism. You are never always right, you're a Napoleonic pig!' Scott gestured all around him at the mangled train. He also took in where the crater had been made in the first carriage. *It only makes me go mad, mad as a hat trick.* 'Doesn't all this satisfy you? I don't need to be corrected by people like you. Now don't give me your peanuts in a tin, I'll just throw them back at you and tin as well right in your face.'

Jane cowered down on the floor. Looking up she could see the other survivor standing next to her. Paul was also pretty much at the bitter end of his tether. Scott's words had given him the courage to make a decision of his own accord. Paul carried on scratching at the driver's cab door, while Jane sighed in disarray.

CHAPTER TEN

Scott checked his watch, as a long time had passed, it felt like a long day. So far it had been a hectic morning getting into this voluntary job than going to his commission shift at London Transport Museum. Further down the train Scott could hear the sound of a train moving. As he listened he dashed down the train. Passing the second carriage he noticed from the rear windows the backlog of carriages were being pulled back. Scott's imagination had an on the spot idea. *The Tube engineers must driving a service train to help us so they can reach the people in the wrecked train more easily.* As Scott looked down at the railway cars he noticed the third carriage was already empty. The people who had been lucky enough to be in the rear carriages had either fled down the tracks or moving back to Kings Cross in the rear carriages. Scott couldn't have even gone with them as he was courageous enough to stay at his station right here between Russell Square and King's Cross. Even had he not encountered Jane; he wouldn't have fled. There was a principle to prove himself to beat the effect of his limitations that was making him a hell's prisoner. As it was his destiny to show the driving force of Aspergers.

'What's going on back there?' asked Nick.

'They're sending a service train to get to us.' said Scott. 'I can tell by sound coming through the tunnel. They wouldn't have let another train come down this way and the Tube engineers are likely to be the only ones coming this way.'

'How would you know that, Scott?' asked Nick.

'I read about years ago and it's still in my long term knowledge.' Said Scott. 'The Underground uses service trains to upgrade the lines, clean the tunnels and maintain the quality of the rails. They are powered by diesel fuel allowing them to operate without the electrified rail, which is useful because we can then walk along the tracks to get out.'

'What, walk out along the tunnels.' said Nick. 'Isn't that dangerous?'

'Not unless you have the Tube staff to guide us out to the next station.' Said Scott. 'It will be nice to get out of here. Although I am quite used to small places like this, I used to lock myself in isolation and enjoy thinking.'

'Might I ask how is that woman you've been arguing with?' said Nick. 'Is she still waving her power all over the place?'

'She's fine.' said Scott. 'I think I've started to set the score with those who let down people with fallible morals. These social justice warriors are useless. They are only ever out to set things straight for their own agenda.'

'There is something I don't get.' Said Nick. 'How could you be able to talk to speak like that? Most autistics are awkward and can't talk to people very well.'

'About a year before I dropped out of school I went in search of a special needs unit that could teach disability awareness and management skills.' Explained Scott. 'But it wasn't a council service though, my neighbour at my previous address was a psychologist and taught me how to cope with my autism and mentor my abilities. Thanks to her I learnt how to converse with people and in doing so I learnt about techniques in debating and rebelling.'

'Rebelling!'

'Yes that's right, I had a good, brilliant imagination and through this program of behavioural training I learnt to break away and think independently from other people, rather than be told to think of myself and know my place as a mentally retarded cripple by the establishment.' Then he broke off and changed subject. 'Hang on, I just remembered.'

'What?' said Nick.

'That blast should have blasted the soot and dust right up into the tunnels.' Said Scott.

'What are you talking about?' asked Nick.

'Well these tunnels. They've been around for over a hundred and sixty years.'

'You are very observant but what's that got to do with anything?'

'Well that fans must have been switched on to remove the congestion and that would explain why there isn't much dust flying around. So when it comes to leaving the train we won't have to worry about breathing problems.' Scott scrambled across back to the front carriage, as if a siren had gone off activating his alertness. H's energy has suddenly exploded into a burst of action. With an excitement that could wake them out of unconsciousness he jumped back to pass the word. 'Right now then, there is hope on its way. They've just sent in a service train and there should be the medics coming along as well. Hold on, they're almost here.'

Scott knelt beside an elderly man who had just come through. Born blind before the accident he hadn't been able to see what was happened. An advantage which for him worked better than actually getting blinded in the disaster. 'What happened? I couldn't see it, as you'll notice how I was before the accident. Tell me what happened?'

'There was a bomb on the underground.' said Scott. 'Some suicidal poor fellow suffered as a result of injustice. That bloody legal fanatic with no conscious failed him and made us suffer and divide us on mental issues.'

'What about my dog?' he asked. 'Where's Scott?'

'Now there's a funny thing, we both share the same name.' Scott looked for the guide dog, as he noticed the torn metal lead provided no trouble in finding it. *Right the man's lead is facing this way so the explosion must have fl -* It was right near the rear door where the old man had been standing with his back to the front. As Scott took the animal's corpse up in his hands he looked upon it totally disgusted. Scott calmly kept his anxiety up about the dog's bodily hair, which was soaked in blood like a dipped sponge with spikes protruding through it's body. This was one of the horrors that had been an image that he'd seen on the TV last year. *The kind of things that lead to this kind of devastation is segregation, as well as negligence. Harbouring evil thoughts and being ignored while the being laid over with a blanket of privileges and pleasurable activities to hide the problem. It's no wonder anyone listens. Not just Orwell, this is Huxley's vision as well. But unlike the selfish, pathetic patronising do gooders I am not insufferable to their arrogance.* The backlash had come and Scott was mindful of the enemy of the peace within the community. *What the hell are we fighting for?* 'Just listen for once and recognise that the freedom to be wrong does not justify doing wrong for others. I just want to shout louder and louder.' Scott was not ashamed to say his thoughts out loud.

Back in the first carriage he went to the blind old man. 'I'm sorry, but it looks like as if I'm going to have to lead you out of here.' said Scott before solemnly moving him to rest on a seat. 'You'll have to wait here a minute until we can move out.' said Scott.

'That's interesting. I didn't know mental bread baskets were sympathetic. Usually they are selfish and can act like greedy pigs.' Jane arrogantly butted in. She looked at Scott like a demonic missionary. Scott compared her expression like she was trying to shun him out of this Earthly existence.

'Well some of them are, but that's only because they are spoiled with the welfare you hand to them.' said Scott. 'Sometimes you give them so much that they become gold diggers. I had a girl from my support group who was showered and sugercoated in a liberal way that she become like a spoiled princess. She's a wheelchair user and she got so much care she treated it like a form of pampering. I however didn't accept anything like that because I wanted something better than the average disabled person who wouldn't even try to find something better than a charitable provision. That's why I am not stupid or blinded by my privileges. You should give the disabled what they ask for to make something productive and helpful, not something that you need out of them of think what they need.'

'Poor pathetic twat.' Said Jane. 'You need a bloody checkover with a doctor, I'd bring that support group of yours to a charge of turning out a crazy psycho, just like that one who tried to kill me.'

'What would you know what good a mental health person is capable of giving to this world.' Said Scott. 'But because of the politically correct nature of the government and the socialist's and liberal's attitude on disablement they have a cotton wool approach to dealing with them rather than listening to what is required of the government to provide for them. I think they should listen to people like me to...'

'Political correctness is there to protect us...' interrupted Jane.

'Now just being a complacent pig.' Said Scott.

'If we stop people committing the evils of society by arming disablement with defensive acts of law, then people will not think prejudice thoughts about you. Besides if I gave you special rights to stand up for yourself then there's no telling what kind of chaos you'd bring. You'd probably destroy us with your craziness.'

'I might be bloody crazy, but that's my best quality.' Said Scott. 'Most geniuses in art and science are believed to possess some form of mentality.' Then Scott returned to make another point. 'Thought control is not good. Do you think the way racial equality laws stand for minority groups by stopping people thinking prejudice thoughts is the right way? That's a time bomb for segregation. It is tantamount to undermining democracy. Democracy and civil nationalism works by listening to it's critics and taken account of it's actions. It understands that all people are different in nature and that we need to accept all classes of citizens.'

'Well some races and groups are more superior to others.' said Jane. 'Considering your attitude to people with race you most probably have racist thoughts. Such hypocrisy, you like mixing with people but...'

'I know when I'm being racist Jane Glouster.' Said Scott. 'What those who call me racist don't understand is their own isms towards others. Social justice are useless because they never really fight for equality at all, just for their own agenda and the groups they represent. They focus only on arming minorities and groups against normal ordinary people instead of creating constructive ways to make a civilised power share of society. I don't want to leave out any minority group, I want to collaborate with them to create something prosperous and happy for all classes of citizens.'

'And have you got an ism?' asked Jane.

'Oh yes, it's an ism that also applies to able bodied people as well.' Said Scott. 'Abled people whom you refuse to allow to develop themselves and create a better, prosperous country that can rid the country of discourse and discontent. That is ableism, and yes not all people agree with me but the freedom to do whatever you want is worth fighting for than being shackled by liberals who are illiberal in their thinking.'

Scott turned to see that Paul had been overhearing their conversation. He nodded in agreement, fed up with his suffering. 'That's a good argument, came straight from the heart.'

'Oh yes I think it works.' Said Scott. 'The fate of human   dignity.'

CHAPTER ELEVEN

Scott's super sensitivity was trained on the tunnels, having poked his head through the broken doors. He listened out carefully for the sound of the Tube engineers and the service train coming down the line. *Providing that ignorant PC culture hasn't caused a problem with procedures, then that train should be here soon. Let's hope that hasn't taken away decency and made things difficult for us.* All Scott ears could pick up were the tinny hollering from down the tracks, where the trains made a rattle like an intro beat. *They must know we are stuck in the tunnel now. The question is how do they intend to do it?*

Scott turned to see a blonde girl who he hadn't paid much attention to notice. Earlier he had seen her crawling on the floor. But Scott felt that she was capable of tending to a victim, which he assumed she was doing. Until now, she needed his help. 'Excuse me. About what you said earlier.

I'm sorry to say this, but I think I've got a cracked rib.'

Scott asked. 'And you are?'

'I'm Sarah; I'm...like I said I can't walk down those tunnels. I think I've got a cracked rib where I hit the vestibule wall. Besides I've got a thing about rodents.'

'You needn't bother' said Scott. 'They are not here.

'Are you sure.' Sarah's whitened face was totally unclear for Scott's recognition. All he could do was listen to her concerns.

'It's a myth that rats scurry in the tunnels of subway stations.' Scott tried to reassure Sarah the best he could, but without emotion. And so once again he started to elaborate on his knowledge. 'Rats wouldn't even be in subway tunnels. The electrified tracks make it too dangerous for them. They'd get electrocuted if they even tried to make the dark tunnels their home. They actually scurry around the stations where there are sources of food for them to gather from the rubbish bins and litter.'

'What so every time I get the morning train there's likely to be vermin around the platforms?' asked Sarah.

'Yes there is.' Said Scott. 'But don't worry I'm sure your beauty would terrify them into a corner.'

'Well thank you Scott, it is Scott isn't it?' asked Sarah.

'Yes that's right.'

'Great.' Said Sarah, amazed at Scott's usefulness. 'If you know so well then you can tell me what else I might bump into when we go in there?'

'I can, but I'm sure how they are going to come and rescue us unless they follow normal procedure.' said Scott. Looking at his watch, he said 'We must've been down here for more than an hour now.'

'You've got a gift.' said Sarah. 'How come you're such an expert on railway operations?'

'I've got a magical ability with my disability, ASD.' said Scott. 'That's autistic spectrum disorder, which I'm sure your probably aware is a curious kind of autism.'

'Well I don't know much about autism.' said Sarah. 'I've got a friend who has a son with that condition. How does it affect you?'

'Well...I suppose it affects my mood and development but doesn't affect my intelligence. You might think of me as the many people do about autism that we are vulnerable and require constant care and attention. Well that's not true. I don't need a welfare officer. I want to show the world that not all people are created in the same way as each other and that we need to respect the difference and adjust to each other's way of thinking. Just because I have a neurological condition that's no reason to exclude me. I have shown great abilities in the last hour that you and some of the other people here have received from me. I have reassured you, tended to your wounds, shared my knowledge that proves something positive. Except that it's a shame that the evil witch over there sees me in a negative way that I should be shunted from existence. And it's because of the stigma and the way the law says how disabled people should be treated according to their inactivity that my creativity and special abilities are dismissed.'

'What are those special abilities?' asked Sarah.

'I'm not sure if I can define it in a way that you'd think of it as a superpower, which of course it isn't.' said Scott in a frank manner. 'Each and every one on the spectrum possesses something special, so in some way they have their own individual powers. In my case I have an incredible knowledge and infinite wisdom. I have tried to use my abilities as an activist or to the benefit of an employer. But it's a struggle to sell myself effectively, because they don't get it.

They don't see a creative intellectual person, only a prized cabbage. Everybody is a genius, but if you judge people by their disabilities they will live out their whole lives believing they are hopeless, useless cripples and spastics.'

'Ohh God!' said Sarah looking shocked.

'Oh yes, that's right you heard it coming from a disabled person.' Said Scott. 'A person who lives with it and knows how to describe it, instead of a layer of government that insists on political correctness before trying to advance people based on the abilities they have and what benefit they have for society.'

'That's awful.' Said Sarah. 'I can't believe that someone like you would have to put up with that. You're a smart man. You'd be great using your intelligence to stand up for us in this situation.'

'Thank You.' Said Scott.

'You must be very articulate with words.' Said Sarah.

'A person who is articulate who masters words commands power.' Said Scott. 'I learnt that from my journalism course. If you have a strong use of words you can survive political poison that crushes independent thought. My mode of speech might be a bit one sided, but that about as much as I can relay my views.'

'You're a journalist?' said Sarah.

'A travel writer actually, I'm not into that news reporting type journalism. I am not interested in those types of things that involve confrontation. I prefer investigative journalism which allows me to combine my love of travel and expressing my imagination through writing.' Then he turned to look at Jane who he could see was up to no good yet again.

Jane was now berating at the door to the front of train, to get the driver's attention. It is not known if he is there or just unconscious but she was slamming her hands on the door in the first carriage like a badly behaved crazy lady who gives her own profession a bad name. 'Come on wake up, I have had enough of this hellhole here.' She said. 'Unless your unconscious then it's a bad way that TfL couldn't beef up security, never mind you.' Then she relented and let back. 'Must be dead, how many more selfish bastards are there in this world that disrupt our daily activities.' Then she turned to see Scott watching her. 'Oh look, it's a pyscho-bomb. Are you going to let off or have a meltdown?'

'Don't say that.' Said Scott. 'Have you no shame. You discredit a mentally ill man, criminalise mental health and now I find you taunting what could be a corpse.'

'It's no different.' Said Jane belatedly. 'I find that you can speak your mind when nobody is listening. Saying it like it is better, even if you are in a well-respected profession.'

'What, you think the fact that you practice law gives you a privilege to denounce people who don't think alike you?' said Scott. 'You might be one of the elite, but you are not an overlord or a superior species to the lower orders of society.'

'Oh please, what would you know?' Then she turned into an insulting. 'That man who tried to kill us today was a freak with a grudge against ordinary people. He was a dangerous as he was a bread basket.'

Scott started to build up with anger and realised his own strength could knock out a villain if he used it correctly. *I'd better not kill her, I'm not giving her the satisfaction of turning me into an inhuman creature, I'll beat her until she knows what prejudice really feels like.* 'Tell me when you social liberalists fight for equality how do you choose which person deserves the most rights and liberties? Don't you know that when you grant rights they come with responsibilities, not special privileges to unleash their contempt on other people. Your priorities are all wrong. I want to live in a world where differences are accepted on a mutual common acceptance of one another in a civilised nation.'

'And what does that mean?'

'It means not having the freedom to commit acts of injustice towards each other so that a black man has a right to beat up a disabled man, a lesbian can firebomb a Christian rights group and a white man doesn't have to put up with intimidation with an aggressive Asian neighbour. How do you expect me as a mental health person to have a peaceful right of existence when there is chaos caused by people like you!'

'Ridiculous, you are.' Said Jane rhetorically. 'Why should I even listen to an addled brained prat like you? You have become a burden for me and ought to be sectioned. No community deserves to look up to you with negative thoughts like a big fucking retard!'

At this point Scott unleased his fury. He pulled his fist back and struck several quick blows right across her person. Jane fell to the floor with her chest hitting a suitcase on the way down. Her ribs cracked and she lay on the floor she turned herself over to look up at Scott. She giggled as he looked down on her with his stern face. 'My God.' Said Scott. 'Even in defeat your still laughing. I suppose your happy that your injuries have given you a compensation bonus, you filthy profiteering prat.'

'What are differences between you and me, my perjury puppet.'

'Oh please.' Said Scott. 'I'm not a puppet, I am not a cabbage, I am not a psychopath, I am high functioning autistic and an essential piece of the puzzle.'

The Conservativism Cause with Rebel Autistics

Right now you would most probably have come to find this story to be well written but has a dark, twisted turn of events as my lead character Scott Hardy turns into a creature of cunning and vengeance. That was in the first edition where he got into a fight with Jane Glouster and knocked her unconscious, but in this new updated edition the fight results in an injury. This rewrite happened because I had to let Scott have an opportunity to prove himself even to his oppressors, that way there would be a hope filled uprising for autism. I haven't made him out to be a devilish, evil disabled person whose mental issues mean that this story is showing the negative aspects of being mentally disabled. That was not the intention. It's actually to make out a serious issue about disablement that I wanted to use my autism for a force for good where the left, the socialists and liberal elite where suppressing my abilities to show my good qualities.

A while ago I started writing for an online newspaper called United Politics (unitedpolitics.uk) which is an online newspaper for people of all views from all parties.

Recently there has been a resurgence in right wing thinking across the political spectrum from ordinary people who feel that they are being suppressed by an overbearing collective of thinkers who demonise those who don't think alike them in an unfair and anti-democratic way. This is known as populism. I wrote a piece for that paper where I explained how I as a disabled person with autism can hold right wing views and what differences there are between attitudes to disablement on the right and the left. In it I made a number of remarks about how I am a proud right wing aspie and with this book I am expanding on that story.

 First, not all disabled people are incapable of achieving anything, defeated and vulnerable to the world's social problems. They are just as capable of being able to fit in with the world and can make something better for the world. There are two types of disabled people. The ones who are welfare and social security benefit recipients who are likely to be left wing. These are the kind who vote Labour, Liberal Democrats and other socialist and liberal parties. Preaching for compassion for the weak in a state of economic incapability who think of themselves as victims of oppression in need of sympathy. Their vote for Labour is just so that they can keep the taps turned on so that they can ensure that their tax payer dependent welfare handouts are enough to keep them healthy. That way they can keep the public sector gravy train rolling. That is not my type. It is this stereotype of disabled people that is often circulated in the mainstream.

Earlier I told of the stories of charities and how their support for the disabled including autism isn't always well directed. There are some charities that devalue the usefulness of the disabled by marketing them as 'second handers'. People whose impairments make them dependent on the services other people. This basic need gives them the idea that autistics are parasites, in the sense that their disabilities make them look like they are suffering a disease like cancer or AIDS.

Autism Speaks is a charity that uses this kind of image for people with autism. There are many autistics who disagree with Autism Speaks and other charities like it. We see it as dehumanizing autism to get people to donate to their causes. Most of the money that Autism Speaks has doesn't even go on autism support services for families. Only 4% of it's budget goes on family services. 44% of it's budget goes on research into autism. But that research does not constitute improving living standards and quality of life for autistic people. It involves causation and prevention of autism like finding a cure for autism and ways to detect it in foetuses to encourage abortions of disablement. It encourages the idea that it is better to be dead than risk getting autism and that for me is a hateful way of raising awareness.

Autism Speaks doesn't have many actual autistics on it's Board of Directors. This is a frequent problem amongst charity organisations. They act like they are a collective of altruists who speak up for second handers. Many disabled people find this counter productive and prejudiced towards them. They are not after awareness, they are after acceptance. The people of autism don't want other people to live for them, they want to be accepted as individuals who have a right of independence.

I am of a kind that believes that disablement should not be accepted as a weakness or defeat. To me a disability like autism or Aspergers has some good qualities that can be useful to an employer or even for society. They are very honest and noble people with a good attitude despite their lax social abilities. As an aspie I have a very strong capable mind that can retain information and recall it in a unique way, which is great for focusing on a particular task or routine. Some people often liken this mental ability to be like that of Dustin Hoffman's character in the film Rain Man. That's not true, not all autistic people can retain information like that. I can't handle numbers in that gifted way that he portrayed a savant. Many autistics do have terrific memories for their passions though. They are often in tune with the details of their interests just as I am with my many passions. My fascination with the world is all about exploring beyond boundaries. I started off in life with only one specific interest but as I matured I started to develop an interest in many other things. However although I like to be passionate about many things I am only able to make one of them useful for providing me with a skillset that I can excel in. That's what many autistics can do in nature. It's one useful ability that we take great pride in. There isn't a weakness in our character that can make us a liability to an employer. I once took a psychometric test for an employee profile study where I was described as 'a precise individual who combines perfectionism with logic'.

 Autistic people are capable of looking at people without being judgemental. Instead we look into discovering real people. I go in search of the actual character of a person or place rather than rely on something typical about the person. Even I am not a judgemental person as I want to be able to integrate with other people and learn about them and see what makes them unique. And because people with autism have certain communication and relationship difficulties they don't waste their time with mind games. Neither do they have hidden agendas and they cut straight to the point about what they want out of life. When it comes to materialism autistics don't have an issue with a person's taste in brands, hairstyles, choice of designer or anything to do with consumerism. A lot of them base their taste in fashion based on practicality and the likeness of an item to their own personal interests. Whereas a normal person would swear by a brand of clothing like a designer shirt I would choose a shirt based on whether I like the colour or the texture of the shirt. People with autism are also a force for good in the world. Their special abilities create opportunities for others that are not on the autistic spectrum with a profound positive impact. I am among one of them as I am already in the process of making something happen right now. I am running a campaign to make archery a core sport in the Commonwealth Games and I have been pressing this campaign into the agenda of the Commonwealth Games Federation. It will only be a matter of time until I develop the opportunities for many archers to better themselves and to give new opportunities for the archery industry.

I have been a Conservative voter and supporter all my life. Although the left and the disability charities often claim that the Tories and the right don't care for disablement with their supposed axe grinding on public services for me they show a great deal of care because they provide opportunities and forms of freedom for disabled people. I accept that my welfare benefits do get cut eventually but to me disability benefits are like 'peanuts in a poor man's tin'. I find that patronising as if I have been punished for a crime that I did not commit, as if I am all worth for nothing other than being a prized cabbage rolling down a street on a socialist vegetable stall. If any vegetable I consider myself to be a smart carrot who is full of life, talent and ability. The capitalists

Conservatives believe that the ability to generate wealth doesn't know any barriers. It is a creative and familiar practice that is lively, human and sociable. It's not a wicked evil set that is harsh and disregards disabled people as a waste, but acceptable to people of all walks of life regardless of their ability. Of course there are some inequalities in wealth creation but those are the ones who dismiss the helpful and productive means to achieve it. I believe that however unequal in nature all creatures were created, we should accept all classes of citizens.

I started to become a politically active person when I started to feel become fed up with the lack of direction and sense of purpose of the New Labour government and the metropolitan liberal elite. That was when the novella was first published in 2005. Back then the attitude of liberal ideas had become so extreme that their critics were silenced with a doctrine that made them feel like they were punished for something that they did not commit. As a disabled person I was getting a lot of privileges and rights of access to which was one of the core objectives of the New Labour mission at the time. They wanted to embrace diversity as part of a post-socialist makeover that showed people that they were not anti-progressive towards economic development as they had been during their 16 years in opposition against the Thatcher and Major Tory governments. However when you fight for equality you don't always appease everyone. In the history of civil rights movements one group always seems to get more rights than the other group within the movement.

 When the civil rights movement started it's emphasis was more on the rights and equality of blacks, woman and homosexuals in mainstream society. Later it splintered into different factions when some of the groups felt that they were being left out. Disabilities didn't get their own charter for equality until 1995 with the Disability Discrimination Act enforced by John Major's Conservative government in 1995. So I think it's fair to say that the Conservatives are not as uncaring as many people think. It was them who created the first law to embrace diversity and equality. All New Labour did was charge through all these equality laws by amalgamating them into one big one. This one was the Equality Act 2010 and that was more focused on political correctness rather than acceptance of difference.

Socialists and equality campaigners often criticise the right for being uncaring and prejudiced towards the lower classes as well the mentally ill. But if you look at this Conservative right wing law there is compassion for the poor and vulnerable. It's just that the left and the right have different priorities over how and who they care. The left believe that all the disabled are incapable and should be granted a lifetime of state provided care whilst the right believe the disabled should have an opportunity to better themselves in life and fulfil what they can achieve with the useful abilities of their disabilities. If that's being positive about disablement, then roll on.

I suppose some of you may think that I am an exception in the autism community for siding with the right. Well I am not, I'm in a minority of right wing disabled people. I have a friend at Essex University who is a fellow Tory in the university Conservative Future society and another who is in the UKIP society and led the Colchester branch of Vote Leave in the European Union referendum campaign, of which I helped to support and campaign through blogging and canvassing as an active Brexiteer. I wanted Britain to leave the EU ever since I became an

Eurosceptic in my teens when I saw the powerful and outrageous bureaucracy and meddling the EU had on it's member states. Among them was a vast number of extreme protectionist policies that forbade development on scientific research and innovation. Including aggressively forcing environmental laws on the continent that made a lot of people feel that they were being persecuted for trying to live in a healthy sustainable way. There was also several rights and regulations it had on the development and opportunities for people with disabilities which were crippling and withholding my own aspirations. Such aspirations as sustaining valuable relations with countries that the EU denies me the right to choose my own destination to trade with for business and political affairs.

The conservative philosophy and the party appeals to me because I am passionate about international relations with other countries for economic and peaceful cooperation, capitalism for producing equal wealth and prosperity for the country and the aspirations of ordinary people, localised governments to allow communities to handle their own interests at heart and a celebration of individual achievements that bring goodness to the country. The conservative ideals are also about developing new innovations in science and technology as well. With the free markets and capitalism business is able to make money from new technology and develop new ideas and systems that people will live with and work with. It is a great philosophy that puts aspiring and good able bodied autistics like me liberalised and advanced to do something that puts value on British society.

I have to admit that for a while I was a moderate Labour supporter but that was at a time. But at that time, I didn't properly understand how my disability works. Although I am a clever person I wasn't always good at school and I didn't accept my diagnoses that well. This is where I will be sharing you my story about my struggle with autism and how I came to be right wing.

When I talk of autism and Aspergers I refer to each other interchangeably as they are closely related to each other. Some people talk of them as different things but being that Aspergers is on the autistic spectrum I accept that I am both autistic and aspergic. Some people in the medical profession still dispute the differences in clinical and academic circles. But the widely accepted definition is that they are grouped into the categorical term Autistic Spectrum Disorder. So for that reason sometimes it's okay to speak of autism and Aspergers as ASD instead.

 I was diagnosed with Aspergers at age 9 but I didn't accept it all. At that point in time having a disability was like a death sentence. I saw it as a weakness that made me doomed to live out my life with no purpose or sense of existence. At the time attitudes to disability were changing and it came in part to a country that was now celebrating diversity and accepting minority groups which included disabled people. But the system that I was growing up in wasn't right for me as an autistic person. By then I had just started secondary school and I had a place in an all-inclusive community school in Bethnal Green. At that time there were only specialist schools in place and the concept of making special provisions for disabled pupils was still in it's infancy. The choices that I had were limited and despite the DDA I still felt discriminated and patronised by my teachers and social workers who thought that I was never going to amount to much. My parents were worried about me too and they struggled to find the right treatment for my disability. The services we had were lacking in anything constructive or positive.

In my parent's time disabled people were rarely seen in society and most of them had virtually no place in society. They believed that I was likely to follow in this path as the rules of equality were not rightfully placed for giving me a decent standing in society. The rules of equality for disabled people at this point in time go like this:

1. All disabled people are alike
2. Disabled people are hideous and revolting
3. All disabled people have no usefulness in society and should not be seen nor heard

Today this kind of discrimination and attitudes to disabled people would be totally unwelcomed. Anyone who lived in Britain before the DDA came into force would know that it was a pity that disabled people including those with autism could not have had their own place in society. Back then disabled people had opportunities according to how employers and schools were able to provide for them. A school could dismiss a child if they were not performing well and an employer could fire a disabled person because they couldn't work effectively with the job they had been assigned. It was this discrimination that social justice campaigners were committed to fight for their rightful place in society. There were some forms of employment available to disabled people in which they had to earn the right to receive handouts in a manner similar to that of community service, as if they were being punished for a crime they did not commit.

Despite my diagnoses and refusal to accept my condition I was aware that I appeared to be mentally different to the other pupils. But still I didn't want to accept it. However, as a disabled person I was supposed to receive special treatment so that I could function in a normal way so that I could manage the effect that my incurable impairment had on my day to day routine. But I never really got those kind of provisions. My community school was a horrible place to get an education. The way community schools work is that they have no connections to business or enterprise so there are no means of showing pupils how to get ahead in the real world.

From day one it looked like I had been set up to fail. The school's study support services were inadequate and lacking in direction. All they did to help assist me was sit beside me in the classroom and watch over my teaching and see that I was paying attention to the schoolwork like an animal being processed for testing. They were so obsessed with making sure that I did well in school they gave no consideration for my safety or my aspirations. I got no disability management programme or social skills training. This is a school where you are told what to think rather than how to think. It feeds you with chronic fear as it reduces your belief in reason and logic as impotent. It stunts a child's intelligence leading him to grow up and life is an irrational chaos that cannot be dealt with.

The kind of education that creates a society seen in the world of Atlas Shrugged that led to the giants of industry and invention to go on strike and leave the country to suffer. I put my own good behaviour on strike by refusing to put up with this chaotic and disorganised institution. I did not want to succeed for their sake to show that they were proud of themselves. They could not break me to think like them.

It was so politically correct here that I wasn't even allowed to try and fit in and let my Aspergers be an excuse to isolate myself. It was like being in a culture of segregation where you had your rights to be alienated from strangers and kept outside the mainstream. I wanted to mix with people but there was an atmosphere of hostility towards each other. If this is how the left think of diversity then they have an illness of the mind towards others. But being kept out of the mainstream was only part of what made me lose all faith in the left and socialism and their sense of care towards disablement.

The school wasn't even as autism friendly as it appeared to be disability friendly. Occasionally the classes I was in were loud and full of so much noise no work was ever done by half the class. Sometimes we had lessons cancelled because of disruptive behaviour and some classes were wasted with hollering going on. This school had a culture of tolerance towards stupidity and idleness. This is a place for people who have no passion and no purpose.

I often complained to my tutors and their response was 'just ignore it!'. It was so pathetic that I likened it to a cattle farm. That's how community schools work, they don't expect you to succeed they expect you to excel at your right to an education. Any life's goals you have are irrelevant. In fact failing grades didn't even exist here, you could get a good mark even if you turned up. Looking back at this experience I can only say that this schooling wasn't really worth anything. It was perhaps the biggest waste of my life and a number of opportunities were lost.

During the New Labour years there were tales of dumbing down the content and quality of teaching and schools. Well my case is an example of just how patronising these social justice warriors and diversity embracing Labour supporters can be. Their idea of showing care and equality is to grant you with privileges that make you incompetent and unproductive. They are not interested in what you want to be, but rather what you can achieve to show that they are making progress in getting people to accept you. This system was killing creativity, individuality and being intellectually abusive. It also stopped people from thinking critically leaving them with no idea of how to improve their situation.

Socialist campaigners believe that we shouldn't expect disabled people like myself to be capable of being able and achieving something with ourselves but accept the weaknesses of our disabilities and use that as an excuse to dismiss individual achievements. I totally disagree with this. For me all forms of life were created unequal in nature and we should accept all classes of citizens. I expect you to accept me for the strengths and abilities for what greatness I can bring to society.

After suffering a terrible education, I left with no useful qualifications or any understanding of mental health management. I spent the next few years afterwards signing on at the jobcentre and selectively forced to apply for certain types of jobs where I stuck in an everlasting catch-22 situation. These jobs that they made me apply for were jobs where I should not have any interaction with other people. The specialist consultants who I went to insisted in looking for realistic job goals. Their definition of realistic job goals was to not try to achieve an ambition, but to accept that I was a write off from mainstream employment opportunities and go into work as a low skilled jobseeker. Most disabled people that I have known in the past find themselves working as gardeners, office clerks, care home attendants, and charity shop assistants. It's like a segregated work system that is dismissive of a disabled person's talents making them feel like this all they have in life. It was so horrible for them to belittle me like this it mentally crippled me and made me think negatively about my disability. How can I feel positive about my autism when I am made to think less of myself?

I never even got any of those jobs at all because my apparent lack of social skills made me psychologically incompetent and unable to sell myself to an employer. Also these low skilled jobs just didn't appeal to me and henceforth I couldn't sell myself to them even if I had to take them. It was very patronising to be looked upon like that, if not beneath my dignity. I am not a job snob, I tried for those jobs, but I just couldn't sell myself to them. I have to love the job and it has to be something that I am capable of doing in order to be able to pass the interview. But I didn't have any experience or the right background to sell myself to them. Something that many jobseekers don't seem to understand these days. What schools today don't teach you is that the bosses don't care about your self-esteem. They expect you to have something good about yourself before you they take you on.

The Equality Act that New Labour implemented in 2010 specified that disabled people should be accepted for what their impairments had done to make them what they are. This is just one type of the endless streams of equality and civil rights rules that they implemented during their time in office. It didn't actually give disabled people an advantage to better themselves, it just gave them an opportunity to put themselves in a position where they could avoid those cobbler's trades they would have done in Ian Dury's time. As a recipient of taxpayer's money on welfare I felt bad about what I was being forced to accept as if I had no real purpose in life but to sit on the sidelines and watch progress being made without a care in the world. I felt like as if I was being taking advantage of by a pestilential leftist who was forcing me to be a puppet of his show.

This lead me to realise something about the left-wing approach to dealing with equality, they only care if you are weak but not strong. These social justice warriors were more patronising than productive. Their idea of showing care and equality is to grant you with privileges instead of opportunities. They are not interested in what you want to be, but rather what you can achieve to show that they are making progress in getting people to accept you. These campaigners believe that we shouldn't expect disabled people like myself to be capable of being able and achieving something with ourselves. They seem more keen on compartmentalising mental health people into a state of weakness. This just reinforces the negative aspects of autism. I prefer to enable myself and that is much more empowering. Something that leftist autistics denounce in an insufferable manner, who side with pathetic patronising do-gooders because they are hateful and negative about disability. They who don't have faith in people of mind and strength and are not seeing my own potential.

Of course in today's society we have a system that is tolerant of disablement. This means that we have a new set of rules of equality for disabled people. Rules that have not even been changed for the better. The new rules go like this:

1. All disabled people are alike
2. Disabled people are helpless, vulnerable and defeated

3. Disabled people need to accept the limitations of their impairments and consider themselves incapable of working

I totally disagree with this. For me all forms of life were created unequal in nature and we should accept all classes of citizens. I expect you to accept me for the strengths and abilities for what greatness I can bring to society.

I have been called ungrateful by my peers for refusing to accept the help and support needed for my disability. Well I am not ungrateful it's just that I am fed up with my life's choices and the way that people judge me on the way that disability affects me. I am not asking for sympathy I am asking for an opportunity in life as an aspirational person. Some people have accused me of being resentful of my autism because of my disapproval of their support services and how I behave when trying to integrate with people. I don't resent my autism, I recognise it's usefulness to my intelligence that makes me useful to society. It's just that the people who look down on me reject my intelligence, thinking that I am a second-hand person who needs to rely on other people.

No person in the world with bright ideas deserves a kind of enforced disadvantage in life.

Whereas many disabled people relished the changes in the social engineering department like the Equality and Human Right Commission I was much more interested in making something out of myself. Trevor Phillips, the head of the EHRC talked about his work as the equality commissioner in his documentary called 'Things We Won't Say About Race That Are True'. In this film he reflected on his work by talking about how the mission for equality actually works. Phillips said that the problem with fighting for equality is that you never know who you are fighting for and for what purpose you hope to achieve. In the context of a slave liberated from his master, what freedom is he supposed to have? To achieve real equality, you need to think about the opportunities that come with freedom, not the liberalisation itself. Otherwise what value do we have for disabled people in society that is worthy of giving them freedom and equality?

On a lighter note I would like to share with you a story about what the Conservatives do that appeals to me, especially for the benefit of autistics. Of all that prejudice that I suffered throughout my life there were opportunities that I am able to gain by a helping hand to get on in life. I support capitalism because it knows no prejudice on race, religion, class or disability. It allows me to think for myself and create something for myself and consider my disability in a positive way. It's taught me to think big and be brave and set my own place in the world that I can be triumphant in my ambitions. There are plenty of amazing talents that disabled people have that we must embrace and share with the world, not shunt them into their own space with whatever they need to stay alive.

Of course, the Conservatives do restrict welfare and all forms of public money systematically and I accept my benefit money may be affected. But as a recipient of taxpayer's money I am not happy with my current situation. I don't want to be in a state where I constantly have money thrown at me, I want my abilities to be accepted and for that I don't need sympathy I need acceptance into the mainstream. About 15% of adults with autism are in employment and 79% are unemployed and on welfare that accounts for those who are capable of working. Now when you struggle to get a job you need to consider making something happen for yourself. An actor struggling a job to perform for will write a script for themselves to work in and use their connections to make something for themselves. An inventor with a brilliant grasp of science and ingenuity made redundant from his job will create something to sell to make a fortune. So we need to be taught to look after ourselves and then we can create something better for ourselves than what we would get as welfare claimants and low skilled workers. If I received a large grant, then I would use that to create a business so that I can set myself up to make something better for the world for ordinary people.

The individual freedom of disabled people gives them the power to show how powerful and magnificent they can be. Teach them to be radical thinkers and they will show you the spirit of disablement makes us champions of society. Autistics are revolutionary and gifted in their abilities and they deserve their freedom for the sake of a better world. Conservativism is a philosophy that teaches us to look after and care for the world and the lands that we were brought up in. Socialism and liberalism nowadays seems to be all about inventing ways for the younger generation to exterminate the parasites of their parents just so that they can live their own way with no regard to their own survival. I believe we should be taught how to care for ourselves and with that we will preserve uphold our traditions and culture. Integrating disabled people isn't a kind of forced labour, but a means to show them that we see something good about them. Some of my heroes had autism and they showed some remarkable talents in science and art.

Hans Asperger, the discoverer of autism said that 'For success in science or art, a dash of autism is essential'. Conservatism is a philosophy that promotes economic liberalism, individuality and civic rights and there are plenty of room for autistics in that field. I want to use my abilities and passion for science to promote international trade and development. With the mindset of an autistic person you have a rationale where you combine logic with reason.

The small government stature embraced by conservatism is well suited for autistics because they can only handle one or a few interests with their special abilities. By supporting a democracy in business we can enable disabled people to show just how useful they are providing that ridiculous red tape isn't restricting their development. In conservatism with autism you have a great number of ways in which you can build a better country. If you are a disabled person in a leftist socialist party you get a hand out and get dismissed from your special abilities, if you are a disabled person in a right wing capitalist party you shine like the bright blue beacon to bring hope to the world.

CHAPTER TWELVE

From the driver's cab muffled voices came with the wind like a group of pub crawlers. Scott peered at the door, where the hole the viewfinder used to be, had a bright light beaming onto him. Even with a light that small Scott could feel it like the sun on his face. 'Oi, they've made it.' he said. 'Someone's shining a torch here.' There wasn't much joy in his tone, but the others looked happy enough. *But what about her. What's she going to do?* Scott picked Jane on her feet. 'Come on, I'm going to show you when the disabled are capable of being able'

'What about the blind old man?' asked Sarah.

'Don't you mind me.' he said. 'Those boys from A and E can get me out better than you can. Get going.'

'Of course sir.' smiled Scott. 'Come on, we've got to get going.' Scott's desire for the simple things convinced Sarah, Paul and Nick. But for Sarah the sight of an industrial sector was not an end to her troubles. She looked shaky but Scott barely felt like he could give into other people's fears right now. He just wanted to get them out. *Don't worry people, I'll get you out even if I have to run you down the tracks.* 'Paul, have you managed to unlock that door yet?'

'Not yet.' replied Paul. 'Hang on, I've got an Allen key here. Maybe this will help.'

'Where did you get that from?' asked Jane.

'I had it in my bag to take to work. It might work on this door.' Paul worked hard on the door trying to undo the lock. He managed to turn it and unlock the door with his key. 'At last, now let's see where we are.'

'We know where we are.' Said Sarah. 'I just wish we have a platform to get onto.'

As Paul open the day he looked ahead at the cab. The driver wasn't there; he was standing ahead at the front of the train where salvation awaited them. The front access hatch of the train was open. Just ahead the lighting was far brighter than the emergency lights on the tunnel walls. A sea of faces were coming ahead. Dressed in bright green and yellow high visibility jackets that shorn in the flashlights. Some of them carrying first aid kits for the wounded victims.

'That's got to be fifty - sixty people have down here.' estimated Scott. 'Hold on, what about stretchers?'

'Don't they know that some of these people are not fit to be walking.' said Paul.

'No, it's just that they can't stretchers down here.' said Nick. 'Those rails would probably trap the stretchers as they were running them along.'

'Well are we going, or are we supposed to just stand here and admire a scenery?' said Scott. They stepped off the train through the forward emergency exit and onto the tracks. *What a train journey, I never thought I would get caught up in something like this. Life often doesn't have that many surprises for me.*

As they started walking down the tunnel one of the Engineers approached Scott. 'Excuse me sir, we have to get you lot out. Is there anyone else in the train back there?'

'Lots of them are injured, but we can move these people and I.' Scott was referring to himself and to the others of his 'survival party'. Although he knew what he was talking about the Paramedic misunderstood him.

'So that's all there is then, just you lot.' said the paramedic.

'No!' said Scott. 'I mean these people, oh I see, no it's just us the and the rest of the walking wounded. The rest of the train is full of dead and wounded. It's like a bloodbath among a set of sardines in a tin...only while it's in the dustbin.'

'Are you okay to move out.' Said the Engineer. Because we're gonna have to move you down the tunnel towards Russell Square station.'

'So what's the plan then?' said Nick. 'Why have you pulled the back of the train away if you're coming down from this end?'

'Well they were removing the back carriages to get through to the wreckage and take the other survivors back towards Kings Cross.' Explained the Engineer. Then he looked at Scott who appeared to be the most able bodied to move. 'You could have taken the chance when they pulled the rear back. Why didn't you jump onboard when you had the chance?'

'Well I had to stay and see to it that these others were safe until you arrived.' said Scott. 'Just because I can move doesn't mean I have to let them be alone. Now perhaps you can help us get out. I've had enough of being in a wrecked train as it is.'

'Right then, perhaps you lot could step this way then please.' Said the Engineer, ushering them forward. As the rescue team led the people along the tracks, Scot wondered what was going to happen next. *Thank God I am on the move again. I really needed to stretch my legs. It was boring listening to that witch back there. Oh well at least I can get a rare opportunity to see what it would be like to see what walking along a tube tunnel is like.*

As interested as Scott appeared to be he wanted to be in total charge of his position. *As always I believe I should stick to the routine as it should be. From my point of view these engineers are doing their job. I can only trust them to do it their way this time. Besides I don't want to break into a meltdown or fly into a rage. I'm done with that and I've unleashed my energy on the witch.*

They started to head off down the bleak void of the tunnel. With the bright lights dotted along the tunnel like fairy lights it looked like a corridor to safety. To Scott though it represented an attentional tunnel. Nick held onto Sarah, petrified but focusing on something relaxing. Her fears hadn't gone far with the trauma of the tube blast among many things on her mind. Scott went up to a passing fireman. 'Just to let you know. I happen to know a lot about tunnels and trains so I will gladly lead these people out myself.'

'I can't let you do that, not on your own.' he insisted.

'Are their paramedics and station staff at Russell Square?' asked Scott. 'This is a one track tunnel, leading directly to Russell Square station, could it be any easier just to follow the route and get out of here!'

'It's alright guv.' said Nick backing Scott up. 'He's well informed and knows pretty much a lot about this rescue stuff.'

'I'm sure he does.' Said the Fireman. 'But if you stick with us then you'll get there safely.'

'Fair enough.' said Scott. Realising their needs we're also a consideration for safety, he wasn't going on a wild chase. They carried onwards to the end.

Jane was now plotting her next move. *What is she up to now? Apart from some malicious claim for victimisation. As a lawyer she'd probably know how to exaggerate claims to feign injury and make a bigger profit.*

Scott's claims of a profit out of a catastrophe reminded him of a charity fundraiser where he was fleeced out of pocket. A few years ago he helped a friend cover a fundraising party. There was a good amount of money raised for the mental health foundation. It was a great cause but he found himself dumbfounded by the costs of the money raised. About 70% of the money raised that night went on covering the costs of the lavish bash, and in the end they ended up making a small donation to keep the charity's running costs going. It was such an appalling practice that he shattered Scott's belief in charity and to that end he refused to get involved in work like that anymore. He likened the way fighting poverty and injustice was like a instrument to stir up sympathy and money for nothing. *Everything about fundraising today is just money raising without solutions. They keep the poor impoverished and displaced so that they can make money out of them.*

That isn't fighting for justice, that's enslavement of the disabled.

'Perhaps I would've been better off with them back in there.' said a jumpy Sarah. 'At least I would've been able to avoid walking along here. It's bloody cold and damp.'

'Now come on Sarah, we're almost there.' said Nick. 'Look at the staff here watching over us. There like our guardian angels.'

'Lucky I'm used to this.' said Scott. 'Sorry if I can't understand your fear Sarah. But it's okay to be fearful. It makes us alert for danger.'

'Well that's really useful.' said Paul. 'It's like a bat in hell.'

The walk along the dark tunnel was enough for claustrophobic proportions. Maybe not for Scott, Nick or Paul but for someone like Sarah she would think there wasn't a chance to get away with her life.

'You were right about the tunnels.' said Sarah nervously tensed. Scott's rapid intuition broke off slowly. He felt angered but calm. 'All this darkness.'

'Darkness?' said Scott. 'What about the emergency lights? It's brighter than looking into an incinerator here.'

'Well that's just what I can't stand.' said Sarah earnestly. 'This is probably the last time I'd use the underground. I only started using it today. There's a long story for you, let me tell you that.'

'Save it till later.' Said Scott. 'There is a much bigger story the world needs to hear. I think the world needs to know that we don't need another terrible catastrophe because of a neglect of mental health.'

CHAPTER THIRTEEN

'So here we are now finally at the destination we were supposed to be.' Said Scott. 'Look at all those staff on the platform. It's nice to see that they've created a makeshift ramp to get us up to the platform.' There was no need for assistance, as they walked up onto the ramp with the greatest of ease. The staff on the platform then stopped to talk to them.

A paramedic in his bright green uniform was standing by a trolley ready to take them up via the lift. 'Hello folks, does anyone need a bed to rest?'

'I think I do.' Said Sarah. 'My legs are killing me and the pain is unbearable.'

'Right come up here then.' Sarah clambered onto the stretcher. The paramedic then started to go over her asking about her health conditions concerning her injuries and then her allergies.

'Okay then we have made it to safety but what about getting up top and into hospital?' asked Scott.

'We have ambulances waiting to take you upstairs.' Said the Paramedic. 'If you follow my directions I'll take you up to them, but first can you tell me what injuries you've sustained.'

'Well I haven't got anything with me, apart from a shocking sound of a blast almost bleeding my ears out.' said Scott.

'I am not sure, I think I might have taken something in my leg.' said Nick. 'I was limping all the way here from the train.'

'As for me it's not anything physical but I think I might have a shocking pain in my head.' Said Paul. 'I don't know if it's trauma or a splitting headache but it's far from the normal hangover from hell.'

Then Jane butted in. 'I need a bloody good surgeon to check me over, I might have cracked ribs.' Said Jane. 'Any chance I can get my private doctor to see me? My face is such a mess.'

'Seriously Jane.' Said Scott. 'We are in need of medical treatment and all you can think of is making sure you get a Harley Street cosmetic surgeon. You can't fix a rib with a make-up brush.'

'Okay then I think we can take all of you with us in one ambulance.' Said the Paramedic. 'If you would like to follow me then I can take you to the lift.'

'Right, this way.' the Station Attendant was ready with her directions. They all went into the lift and went straight up to the ground floor. When they got out they could at last breathe a sigh of relief. The fresh air on their faces made them feel happy like children who had ditched the TV for the great outdoors. Finally with the sun on their faces it was a moment of liberation. *So good to be outside now.*

They were totally speechless. 'My God it's quite an armada out around here.' Said Scott. 'Look at all those emergency service workers, the sound of helicopters overhead and the news crews trying to get information. I suppose they were expecting a bloody mess today.

'A bit like how my shirt ended up this morning.' said Paul.

'That's good, even if I lose I'll be famous.' said Jane. 'Take note because this is going to make a scene if you get your carcass on the news because then the insurance has a nice premium to it.'

'Shut up bitch.' Said Paul. 'You've been throwing your weight around all day.'

'If I ever get told for a reference I am going to bloody destroy your reputation Glouster.' Said Scott. 'I don't like my battles being fought by a publicity whore and a casualty profiteer.'

'Suit yourself, but don't expect me to defend you when you get laid off if you end up being a cripple.' Said Jane sarcastically. 'Come to think of it limbless people are better clients than psychos because they are more thankful.'

'If we don't get her to back down and stay away from the courts, I'm gonna smack her in the mouth just for fun.' Said Scott. Jane moved on ahead out of earshot of the others. 'I've already given her cracked ribs and I think her mouth deserves a stitching.' The others just looked frustrated with angst written all over them. 'I suppose now is the time I can start writing up, namely on how a journey to hospital is more fun than a trip to a museum.'

'Well your skills as a journalist will let you interview the survivors.' said Nick.

'I can interview you guys.' said Scott. 'It's fit enough for print. In fact I can use it to expose her. I wonder if there is any other bad practices I can find on her.'

'Well there you go then.' said Paul.

'Why don't you just write up about your own experiences.' said Sarah. 'That way you would've proved just how good you are. I think you've proven a really good voice to prove positive for disablement.'

'That's true.' put in Scott. 'But where do I begin? I've never investigated something like a disaster before. I'm a travel writer not an undercover reporter.'

'Y' know what, I think you can try it.' said Paul. 'You stood up to her like that and gave her an almighty big whack down there.'

'It certainly showed me what the biggest sewer rat in history looks like.' Said Scott.

They found an ambulance to get into and told the paramedic at the wheel about their situation. '

'Okay then everybody I have my wagon ready to roll.' He said in a ranger like manner. 'Buckle up and we'll make haste.'

'Step on it.' Said his co-driver, after the doors were shut. 'Right everyone okay for a journey.'

'Which hospital are you taking us to?' asked Scott.

'Whitechapel, East London.'

'Oh, that's where I was born.' Said Scott. 'I've been there for treatment probably a dozen times in the past.'

'What was that for?' she asked. 'A childhood illness?'

'No, my mental health issues.'

Scott then looked at the others to see that they were not in the mood for talking. For the rest of the trip it would be better to sit back and rest. After all we haven't really got much to look forward to, apart from rest.

CHAPTER FOURTEEN

They arrived at the hospital and disembarked quickly to be seen by the media who had seen them make their way out of the station on TV. Still anxious to get themselves safely into hospital they barely felt like walking. But Scott was still active without an ounce of tiredness now that he had sat down in the ambulance. 'Hold up' they said. 'Mind how you go.' As he looked behind at them after a few mega paces he realised they weren't catching him up. 'What's wrong?' he said.

'Steady on Scott.' said Sarah. 'We can't exactly play road runner to get into the hospital.'

'Do you think that four injured people still have fit legs?' asked Paul.

'Sorry I was just alone for a minute there and again.' said Scott. 'Alright let's make speed and ease.'

'Speed and ease?' said Paul. 'Who are you joking?'

'Come on let's just get in there.' Said Sarah hastily. They carried on into the reception area where there was a queue of doctors and nurses ready to take them in. They stood there like waiting staff at a service station expecting broken bodies to come though able to repair people on demand. Being that it was a great disaster there was a lot of casualties expected which could only mean that they will be at their busiest than ever before. Scott took to it automatically without expecting someone to talk to him. Following the directions his nurse was giving him, he saw her name tag had Rebecca. He's always had a problem with people that he can barely except others to surround his vision. The world in motion to him is full of pictures and moving descriptions that had to be followed autonomously.

'This way please.' Said Rebecca. 'I'm Rebecca.'

'Yes I know I can see the name on the tag.' Said Scott.

'Your very observant.'

'I'm Scott.'

'Perhaps, you can tell me what happened to you today.' She asked. Scott talked to her about his business today on the train, but she asked him to cut short when he went off a bit on the topic. 'What I was in was a ducking position. I dropped my notebook just seconds before the bomb went off. I had a lucky stroke when it happened and I was still duck and cover when I took the blast.'

'Incredible!' said Rebecca. 'How could that happen. It's like as if you had a sixth sense or something.'

'If anything I think my senses were switched off, I couldn't even feel the heat of the blast.' Said Scott. 'I think my autistic traits may have given me an unusual sensory system. I sometimes go out in the cold and forget to put on a coat.'

'Well I never would have guessed.' Said Rebecca. 'You certainly don't look autistic.'

'My disability isn't really all that visible.' Said Scott. 'Most autistics grow up and as they age their impairment's behavioural patterns fade. I can talk a lot more and read people's faces and I can tell by your face your keeping a bright face despite my injuries.' Scott then looked at himself. He could see where Rebecca has patched him up with a few bandages and plasters. 'It looks like I made relatively unscathed. I haven't got to come back for a check-up or anything have I?'

'Not quite, but I will book you into an appointment just to be on the safe side.' Said Rebecca. 'I think you'll be able to take those bandages off after a few weeks. Hey, being that you're a writer maybe you could make a story about this adventure you had.'

'I could, but there is a much bigger story that needs to be told.' Said Scott.

'What's that all about then?' said Rebecca.

'I need to prove a point positive.' Said Scott. So he made his way out of the ward and went downstairs to the reception area. He then took in the sight of the other wounded coming into the hospital who were in agony. Some of them unconscious as they were being carted into the wards on stretchers. 'What kind of sick psycho could do this?' shouted one angry woman. 'You don't if anyone's safe on the public transport these days. Anyone with a deranged head should not be allowed into society. They can be radicalised and made a danger to us all.'

All these remarks about mental health were making it upsetting for Scott. *These people have only suffered because of a segregationist attitude to diversity. The whole point of embracing diversity is to accept the best of difference, it's not to subvert people into thinking they need to accept something they oppose.* It was depressing to see people make these remarks, but he did treat or see it as hateful towards mental health, he saw it as a result of a vilification owing to having other people's problems imposed on them. *I don't want my problems causing this, I want government and society to recognise the need for improving health. What do they need,*

Scott went outside to see the news crews. He
approached one of them he saw earlier.

'Excuse me can I have a talk with you for the
cameras?' said Scott. 'I think you've got hear what I
have to say.' The newscaster broke off from his
report to speak to Scott.

'Hold on I think I might have a story from one of the
victims.' He said. 'Right okay then.' He placed the
microphone up to Scott.

'I was one of the survivors from the disaster on the
Piccadilly Line. I have to tell you something that I
know from the carnage. The bomber wasn't a
terrorist or even a religious fanatic of any kind. It was
a desperate cry for help from a suicidal man who
tried to take his revenge on a person who
criminalised him.'

'And what makes you say that?'

'I found out from a friend of the bomber who was
travelling with him. The bomber's name was Frank
Craine, a man with a mental health disorder who
committed suicide without thinking about other
people because of the stigma put upon him by a
corrupt woman who was on the train. Craine was a
former employee of a chemical factory whose case
was dismissed in a court last week. The lawyer who
was on the train was Jane Glouster who was with me
on the train and she is now at this hospital. I am

telling you about this because she carried out a miscarriage of justice to criminalise mental health and further stigmatise mental health problems. Had he been better treated the disaster may never have happened at all.'

'It sounds to me like your defending this man Craine.' Said the Newscaster.

'This is not a defence, it's a cry for help that was blown right out of hand and in effect it unleashed a terrible mess all because he was victimised by a greedy corporation. It is just about the same as using a vulnerable person as an instrument of destruction. I am a mental health person, I have autism and I find it very insulting that a person would go out of the way to make the people of my kind a weapon and a timebomb. A bomb that exploded in the face of society caused by a horrible, horrible person. The poor fellow was a man who looked like he was being further isolated from his community and forced into the comfort of a devil. '

'What are you saying he was controlled by a ringleader?'

'No! Not a ringleader, maybe I am not express myself properly here but what I am trying to say to you is that this Glouster woman has taken advantage of a vulnerable man and made a fortune for herself out of another man's problems and the disabled. And I want it on the air that the mental health services of this country are letting people down and shunting them into misery and despair. Shame on the law, shame on those greedy profiteers. I am not a puppet or a timebomb to be used against their opponents. You've got to understand that the mental health has a great deal of contributions and abilities to give to society. That woman in there has given us all a might big headache. And I tell you now I will not be patronised and made to feel a slave to my own impairment.' Scott then turned away, 'Sorry for that but it had to be heard.'

Scott walked back to the hospital and went back to his cubicle. Along the way he got some stares from people who thought he did well. One man high fived him along the way. But to some they felt that he had breached confidentiality. One doctor stopped him in his tracks.

'Do you realise that you've made a mistake of revealing a patient's whereabouts?' he said.

'Quite frankly doctor, I don't give a damn.' Said Scott. 'They can come a sue her, lynch her, or crusade against her for all I care. Now if you'll excuse me I have to find my friends.' Scott walked away and started to do some constructive thinking.

CHAPTER FIFTEEN

Scott went upstairs to find Nick, Sarah and Paul on the ward. 'Excuse me doctor.' asked Scott. 'Can you tell me where I can find the people who I came in with, I just wanted to talk to them?'

'Follow me I'll show you where they are.' He said. 'Can you tell me who they are?'

'Yes, one woman called Sarah and two men called Nick and Paul.'

'I think I have seen them earlier.' Said the doctor. 'They are just around here.' Scott saw them lying in the beds now patched up and resting healthily.

It took a while for the doctors to cross examine everyone on the ward. As soon as they had finished, the leading nurse, stood at the centre at the centre of the room. 'Right, we've done what we can here for now. So I suggest we go down and wait for any more casualties.' She turned, and walked up to Scott. 'Look, I know this must be difficult for you.'

'Oh no, it's actually going quite well.' said Scott.

'Well if you need anything just as the nearest member of our staff?' she said.

'Right okay then.' The Nurse waved her staff to leave the room. 'Listen, if it's not too much trouble can you watch over these people for me.'

'Course I can, I came with them in the first place.' said Scott. The Nurse made a positive gestured as she left the room. Scott turned to see where she was going. 'Most of the staff have probably been called away to other duties.' he said. Closing the doors he sat down beside Sarah. 'Right then. Now guys I think we can settle this with our own story to tell. I've just been out on the forecourt of the hospital explaining to the media what the segregation and shunting of mental health problems into isolation can do.'

'Yes we know.' Said Paul. 'It was on the news only just now. Saw it on the TV screen over there.'

'You made quite a good impression.' Said Nick. 'I must say you handled that statement with dignity.'

'Thank You.' Said Scott. 'Now I think it's time for me to get the exclusives. That's your stories on what you happened to you. If you tell them not only will I have something to write about but there will be something that you can use to prevent the vilification of mental health, build a case to bring down and put Glouster on trial and see to it that you get an opportunity to show accountability to someone who you think is really responsible for this.'

'I could name a number of other people who deserve to ruined.' Said Paul. 'I hope that squeeze every penny out of that witch's piggy bank. Never mind compensation, she deserves to be punished.'

'Well if you let me get my electronic recorder out of my pocket I can save on note taking.' Said Scott. 'Here we go. Nick do you want to go first?'

Scott put the recording apparatus in his top pocket so as to avoid the nurses from seeing him. *One word of a journo in the building and I'm out!* He switched it to record and casually struggled with his tone. 'I'm at the Great Ormond Street Hospital in Central London. Here I'm joined by three of my friends. Now it's not often that I make a lot of new ones but anyway I'm with erm....' he struggled with his first set of questions. '...tell us about yourself Nick and start with your own words.'

'I'm Nick Clough; I was a passenger on the train to Russell Square station. I can only describe today as being one of the most traumatic days of my life. I was on my way to take a trip to the Tower of London. There I was with my back facing the end of the second carriage from the front. I was reading a paper at the time so I wouldn't have seen the blast. All I felt was someone from behind me falling on top of me. That person must have taken the blast and suffered because of it. The next thing that I remember was waking up to a burnt out carriage. It took me a while to take it all in. Then I remember seeing you come to my aid. I think you were a very resourceful person and despite being a mental health person started to reassure me. I have never seen anything like that in a person with an autistic spectrum disorder.'

'Well I suppose that is an example of how able a disabled person can be.' inputted Scott. 'We're not all of the sniffling, quivering wrecks that you see in the general consensus.'

'I suppose it could be like first-hand experience with you. I started to piece myself together again. I tried to stand up and I realised the pain my leg. I had a jagged piece of my flesh blasted away exposing the tendon.' Looking back at his leg, this was now bandaged and patched up with stitches. Nick felt lucky now that he wasn't looking on the inside of his own body. Scott looked too giving himself pointless shivers. *I've always had a burning sensation to avoid acute pains. They wouldn't even make me flinch unless it was small.* Super sensitively aware of his surroundings, he was always on the lookout for where the pain might come from.

'Poor devil, I suppose anyone would like to show their courage with a scar from today's events.' said Scott. 'Or is that just me reciting the scene from the St Crispian's speech in Henry V?'

'Well you don't need one.' said Nick. 'It's right there as a mark of significance and character and distinction.' He pointed to Scott's head, which made him look at the mirror on the desk. Until then he realised what Nick had actually meant.

'You mean my autism.' Said Scott. 'Well thanks. If only the rest of the world could appreciate that then they'd realise what they are missing.' *Thank the Lord I 'am appraised.* 'So erm...what else is there?' Scott tried to think of a suggestive question.

'That's all I can give you for the moment, now.' said Nick. 'Like they say, the rest is history.'

'What about when I had to leap to other people, now surely you remember that thing?' said Scott.

'Well I sat there on the floor like you put me in. When you were gone I just propped myself up onto one of the seats.' Said Nick.

'Then there was the walk along the tunnel.' Said Scott. 'I bet that wasn't strong or very appeasing to be in for you, was it?'

'Well that was just as bad as being in a burnt-out powder cake. The most appeasing sight was having the Sun on my face again.'

'Okay.' Scott spoke into his recorder. 'Survivor Nick Clough, not that many regrets to even think about.'

'How about me.' said Sarah. 'I wanna go next.' Scott went over to her bedside just opposite Nick's. Checking his recorder was still running he began ready with his questionnaire.

'And how about you, I haven't actually got your full name yet.' said a chilled Scott.

'Sarah Padbury, I'm a marketing consultant from Birmingham.'

'Like the accent.' complimented Scott.

'Thank you. And now to get where I was meant to be. I was heading off to work in Covent Garden.' For a split second Sarah's face went grim. 'And actually I haven't managed to phone them that I'm several hours late.'

'This disaster is big news Sarah, don't worry they'd probably have a bit of decency to assume what the worst is. After all you got caught in a major accident, I think they'd understand. You can explain on the phone later.' said Scott.

'I hope so.' Said Sarah. 'One time I took a job and they didn't empathise with my reason for being late when I got caught up in a traffic accident. They were idiots.

'Right, well I can think that doesn't matter now.' said Scott unintentionally stern. 'You can carry on now with your story.'

'I was sitting near the doors, the first set of doors just at the front of the second carriage. My back was facing the doors in the cramped train. I had already got the sensation of the cold glass windows against my back. It was like having a cold shower even as I felt the air seeping through the cracks where the doors slide shut. Then I felt this big shockwave following the explosion blurring my eyesight. Next thing I was thrown against the window pane, narrowly missing the tunnel wall.' Sarah then began to murmur. 'I suppose if I'd grazed myself on that wall with the train moving at that speed then I'd surely be dead.'

'What happened when you realised your injuries?' asked Scott.

'Well I was out for a while, twenty minutes, maybe ten. When I came round I must have thought Oh fuck! My best suit is ruined. But I couldn't really care about it for the moment. All I wanted was a nice comforting set of words that could make me feel whole again.'

Scott could not understand the point of the joke if it was one. *Now this is just why I can't understand humans!*

'You whole?' said Paul cheerfully.

'Yes wholesome and full to bring me out of that misery.' Said Sarah. 'What I was going through was a dark place. Funny how it turns out when I am already in a dark place, a wrecked train in a tunnel. But then there was some solitude when I saw you come to me. A gallant gentlemen with a big brain, but not much of a heart. If you get what I'm saying.'

'It's okay, I get what you mean.' said Scott. 'I might not be very well at expressing my emotions or empathy but I do know how to treat people. And out of that I expect people to understand the way I think and feel, if not my behaviour. I know I have a funny way of expressing myself physically but I am not really interested in reading a person's body language. I try but it's now always good.' Then Scott returned to the story he was after. 'Now as you were saying Sarah.'

'Well as soon as I realised I needed a change of clothes, I felt my back to be full of glass shards just beneath the shoulders. I could feel the linen in my jacket torn where the shards had cut into the flesh, which is why I'm lying here on my front. Is there a mirror there?'

Scott looked on the desk to find a mirror, he found one to hand to Sarah. She turned on her side to hold it against her back so that she could see the injuries. What Sarah found was devastating. Her back was covered with a shower of cuts like whiplash. Touching them at the slightest of narrow margins was enough to make her flinch. In Scott's experience he didn't react that much to a splinter, yet alone a tiny cut. Sarah stroke further to note the bump just around her waist where the bottom of the train's window frame had dented her with a bruise. She put her head on her pillow shattered but dignified. Scott put a hand over her shoulder, determined to watch over her 'til she made it out of hospital. *A job worth doing is another interest worth an obsession, so I'm not leaving my post until they've overcome their pain.*

'You know what I feel right now?' said Sarah.

'What?' asked Scott.

'I feel like as if I've just took the wrong steps in my life and then suddenly I realise I've been plunged into this horrible alien abyss and it's all because...' She tried to think but didn't know what else to expect. '...oh I don't know! What happened to me today?'

'Don't think your defeated.' said Scott. 'However terrible your injuries may be that does not make you a second class citizen. Look at me born differently but I don't feel that makes me unable to fit in or worth hiding from the world. There are plenty of things in this world that can be brought to make a civilisation thrive in harmony and I think you have a part to play in it. Not only do you have civil liberties but you have a responsibility to show you have a place.'

'Come here' said Sarah. 'I want to hug you.' Scott and Sarah hugged each other. 'That's the best and most hopeful thing anyone has ever said about me. There were times when I wished I had cancer because I was never getting anywhere in life. But now having met you I can see that there is a reason to live life to the full.'

'Well I'm glad to hear it.' said a solemn Scott. 'I never really get given hugs unless it's a relative. But I now have a good sense of humour to accept one.'

As Scott moved over to Paul's bedside he motioned without feeling a hint of sadness. 'Well how about you then Paul.' said Scott. 'What's your name, age and business about the tube that got cocked up this morning?' Paul took the recorder from Scott's top pocket like he was his own chat show host. The others looked on amused.

'This is Paul Fielding.' he said it like a cheesy person while getting stuck on his own dialogue like he'd forgotten his script. 'I'm 22 and I'm an art student from North London. I was on my way to the National Portrait Gallery to gather some research and inspiration for my gap year a bit like you Scotty boy.'

'I'm not even at university and no, don't do that.' said Scott. 'It makes it sound like I am picking up a recording of a chat up line.' Nick and Sarah laugh off as Scott sat down beside Paul. Taking the recorder out of his hand and placing it on the bedside table. 'I'll put it here. No one is watching anyway. So go on, carry on with your statement, it's recording all the way.'

'I was kneeling down beside the front of the driver's cab.' he began in a regretful manner.

'So you were in the carriage where the blast happened.' said Scott. 'It's a bloody miracle that you got out alive and well. Most people get blown to smithereens when you're in the wrong place at the wrong time.'

'Quite.' Paul continued. 'I had been getting back to my hotel as I'd been drinking late night in an Islington flat where I hit it off with a bird that shared the place with a friend. You won't believe what state I was in when I left this morning. Bird meaning - '

'Slang for girl, I know.' Scott reminded himself as he'd used the word before.

'Well I won't go into that.' continued Paul. 'So I literally slumped at the door of the driver's cab thinking as if I'd just got home already. I was worse than when I started out here. You can tell by the way I was before I came out of the tunnel. I looked a lot less badly than before I got on the train. I couldn't see the blast because I had my eyes shut so I guess I must've nodded off. But what I do remember is being forced with a shockwave of warm wind up against my face. The last time I opened my eyes was when the train pulled out of King's Cross. It was a packed carriage and the people were all gone in a blur. Shortly after the bang I suppose the thing had sobered me up. I was in a hellhole!.'

'You must have an experience of sleeping in bad places.' Said Scott. 'Do you think your partying is getting too wild?'

'I suppose it is.' said Paul. 'I think I had better learn to start taking things one step at a time. No more partying or booze. Learn to embrace cleansing and save up for something more meaningful.'

'And if we can return to your story.' said Scott.

'As I was saying.' continued Paul. 'I was just sat there at the base of the door unconscious. You could say I was as stiff as a board.'

'I know I saw you in that state when I saw you in the corner. Perhaps you can make your words a bit serious. You are not talking to a stranger in a pub.'

'Alright then.' Said Nick. 'Well to get serious was a bit of trouble. I started to get that desperate feeling of escapism running through my mind. I banged on the door to try and get through to the driver's cab. I had to assume he was dead because of the way I was banging so loud on the door. Then that crazy lady came up to me.'

'Does anyone know where she is?' asked Scott. 'I thought she would be here.'

'I haven't got a clue.' Said Paul. 'She must have gone off somewhere, probably for a ciggy. But what I'll never forget is how you stood up to her. You handled that woman with dignity and the words came straight from your heart like a magnificent crusader. I tell you she is going to get what is coming to her.'

'I have never used my strength like that in a way that I have knocked her out and down to the floor.' Said Scott. 'Most of the time I have used my boxing skills to release stress and anxiety.'

'She certainly made for a good stress ball.' said Paul. 'I am not one to use violence to settle an argument but with a stinking attitude like that she deserved it. I am sure you are a good person, I don't doubt it. Not all mental health people are psychos. Sometimes they have great strengths in situations like that bit they are not freaky bastards that should be locked away. But that's not to say that I could use you as a mad dog to set on someone. You use your intelligence.'

'Well that's settled then.' Said Sarah 'I think we can bring a strong case to settle this crisis and restore harmony in the community. The way some people disregard mental health, it's criminal I tell you. The suicides, the suffering and look what happened when that poor man got physically frightening and blew people up today. It breaks my heart.'

'Don't you worry Sarah.' Said Scott. 'This shall be taken very seriously. By me of course.'

'So what do we do now?' said Sarah.

Positive Impact of Autism on the World

Now that Scott may have proven that a disabled person can have right-wing conservative thoughts and have a useful worthwhile life of opportunity that the left won't honour on prejudiced grounds, I think it's time to look at the positive aspects of autism. So positive that they shine a bright light that acts like a beacon for all the world to hope for.

As an autistic conservative, I can tell you that there are some politicians who are proud to support autism. Some of them are just as supportive of their autistic children. Conservative Canadian MP for Edmonton-Wetaskiwin, Micheal Lake has an autistic son called Jaden and he spoke in his maiden address in 2006 to Parliament about how much he works hard to support his son's mental health and development. Since being elected to Parliament, Lake has made several notable speeches on World Autism Day.

In 2015 he told the Canadian House of Commons of how accepting he was of son's condition and that 'autism brings with it big challenges but if we help his challenges we'd never want to lose the Jaden we have now'. He believes that the more we are accepting of autism into the normal community (i.e. the mainstream) the more we can accept them as accepting all classes of citizens. In which through our fellow citizens we can allow people with autism to thrive.

As a political activist, I can see what he is trying to achieve and make good for the world. I have tried to express myself as a useful and remarkable person to the world but the resources were never there for me to thrive and succeed in my abilities. The focus was always on my limitations and inabilities. The left-wing community services that I had were basically focused on providing me with endless welfare subsidies. Filling my head with the chronic fear of having no imagination and that thought is an illusion. This is typical of a politically correct schooling that gives no concept of the real world by stunting children's brains, reasoning is impotent, and existence is an irrational chaos in which you will have no control over your destiny. There wasn't any hope of a chance to better myself and it reduced my abilities impaired by a state of chronic terror. I wish had the right honourable Mike Lake there with his type of services when I was young. He'd know better for what I could contribute to society because he'd be accepting of my abilities.

 In the snap general election of June 2017 I was very busy in my political activities. The first thing I did was get ready to campaign for a Conservative majority government. At the time the Tories had made several successful campaigns in winning by elections and local council seats in parts of Britain. This led leading members of the cabinet to think that if we called a snap election then maybe we could increase the strength of the government to get a stronger hand in negotiating Brexit. However sadly due to complacency, mismanagement and some terrible disasters that effected the country socially the election didn't turn out the way we expected it. But that's another story. What I got out of that campaign was an opportunity to prove the best of abilities and to show myself off to the country as the autistic conservative.

 I was assigned as an assistant to a ward coordinator called Christine Vickery of the north Romford area. I was so dedicated to the part that I became her right-hand man. It was a great opportunity to work alongside her and to serve a strong, powerful independent woman with a big hearted devotion to people and community. I felt like I had become like a deputy to this part of town.

In doing this I demonstrated just how strong and confident I was as an activist and I learnt the true meaning of campaigning. It's about making something of yourself and challenging your opponents with the strength of your mind and body, it's not about using a cause for promotion of egoism and using your hatred of some problem to stamp out injustice using brute force or hysterical rhetoric. Politics is about people and when I was canvassing with Christine I learnt how to deal with issues face to face. I was a very good listener and I shared my knowledge with the voters and tell them some hidden truths about the way democracy works that are rarely talked about. They were surprised to find an autistic amongst the Conservatives and especially keen to know how I could probably help the government and how the people can help themselves. The reason for this is because of the spitefulness and apathetic attitude to political affairs that run in the daily workings of government and people's understanding of issues. That explains the lack of imagination, creativity and sense of bettering ourselves to advance the country. I can't stand that insufferable defeatism.

Collaboration is the way forward and I think we need to educate ourselves better to take responsibility for our own democracy. If I hadn't taken up this responsibility, then I would have left Romford out of pocket and not put community first. As an example of going above and beyond to prove my autism gave me strength I went to canvass for three other candidates in Colchester, Hornchurch and Upminster, Rainham and Dagenham. Most of them now have good strong people of character standing up for their constituencies of good honest people. And I look forward to communicating ideas with them, specifically for my own interests to improve my quality of life that I can share with others. If autism can make politics and conservatism successful then I can show how valuable I am to the country and to my party. Autistics are incredible creative, critical and innovative individuals. The Conservatives have given me opportunities and help me to discover ways to better myself and share my skills and knowledge with the world. All you'll get out of a party like Labour is a tin of peanuts like a poor beggar with his disability negatively reinforced and made to consider himself vulnerable and defeated. Well I'd rather throw the peanuts and the tin in the face of socialism and liberalism and reject their dogmatic prejudice. All forms of life were created unequal and we should embrace all classes of citizens.

Researchers into autism often claim that Aspergers syndrome can cause an advantage. Instead of seeing the traits in their disability as flaws that need to be corrected we should use them to their advantage in certain spheres. Autism is a neurological condition that affects the way the brain is developing; hence they differ from normal brains. This brain organisation has certain benefits. People with autism can make significant contributions to society in the right environment. Albert Einstein was an example of this. He was believed to be autistic because he displayed plenty of symptoms in his behavioural patterns. Neuroscientists have found that the parts of his brain, which is the only part of his body preserved, are unusually shaped. The region that deals with speech and language is smaller whilst the region that deals with numerical and spatial processing are larger. In fact he had a larger than normal sylvian fissure, which may have explained how he thought visually rather than verbally.

It's interesting for me to understand this because when I was young I was a struggling communicator and an active visual thinker. When I was young I barely spoke and I obsessively had my head in deep thought about the subjects that I was obsessed about like an introvert. As I matured I started to be able to communicate more effectively. Einstein too had a similar development pattern to me. He couldn't speak until he was four and he didn't read until he was seven. His parents and teachers were worried that he was mentally handicapped and that he would never amount to much. Although he was a brilliant theoretical physicist who achieved worldwide fame with the theory of relativity, he never liked school. He was educated by a rote system which stifled his ability to think freely and he often got into trouble with his teachers. He likened his school to barracks and his teachers to lieutenants. He left school a year early with no qualifications to his name. At 17 he tried a second time to get into the Zurich polytechnic and aced it. It was here that he was a rebel with a cause and after he left he spent seven years working as a patent clerk at the Swiss patent office and whilst he was here he devised his famous theory of relativity.

Some autistic people outperform normal people with their exceptional abilities. Not everyone of them possess the same abilities as Einstein but they each have one to their own speciality. They are less likely to misremember anything, as I have had difficulty being forgetful. This skill is particularly useful in my passion for science where I can recall the steps in a visual way. However my mathematical abilities are not as strong as Einstein's. Whereas he mastered calculus that is mostly text based, I can master trigonometry which is mostly illustrated maths. Some autistics are so good at visual based thinking that they can recall text based information in a visual way.

The 1988 film 'Rain Man' put autism into popular culture. It vividly portrays the magnificent abilities of a gifted person with a disability into a heart-warming tale. The film had been based on a real life person who possessed these special abilities called Kim Peek. He had a great mental ability with his way of thinking that he could tell what day of the week a person's birthday was. Now although many autistic people have great learning and thinking abilities not all of them are like that. I haven't got a talent for behaving like a calendar or a quantum computer where I can answer to a complex question on demand.

There are three distinct types of autistic thinkers. Visual thinkers that can be excellent in artistic and imaginary thoughts but can be poor in mathematical puzzles. Einstein said that his maths problems are far greater and that other people should not worry about theirs. Pattern thinkers are another kind who are likely to excel in maths, music and symbolism but are poor at reading and writing. Pattern thinking is also known as design thinking and it can be useful in design-cognitive activities for architectural and civil engineering planning. This is a practical, creative resolution approach that is a very powerful and strong quality in a person with autism. The last one is known as verbal specialist where the person has excellent skills in the art of oratory and rhetoric. They also have a useful ability in writing where they take notes actively and can retain information from lists, timetables, routes and labels. Not like in a pattern style but where there just needs to be words in the form of a set of instructions.

These thinking patterns combined with the other useful traits in a person with autism. Now I think it's time we took a look at some other geniuses from the arts and sciences who are believed to be autistic. They may have been autistic based on the studies of their character and patterns of behaviour. Einstein had such a difficult communication problem that he repeated his sentences until he was seven, insisted that his wife follows a code of conduct and was often a loner at times. He had a saying about loneliness that 'it gives you time to wonder, search for the truth. Have holy curiosity to make your life worth living'.

There are many people who are diagnosed or believed to be autistic whose work has made people's lives worth living. The doctor who first recognised the condition Hans Asperger famously said 'For success in science or art a dash of autism is essential'. Most of these people happen to be scientists and artists. Isaac Newton, James Joyce, Thomas Jefferson, Bill Gates, Charles Darwin, Andy Warhol, Emily Dickinson, Marie Curie, Jane Austen, Abraham Lincoln, Daryl Hannah and Alexandra Graham Bell.

Let's start with one of my heroes of science. Thomas Edison had six months of formal schooling. He was dismissed by a teacher with a note that read: 'Thomas is too stupid to learn anything, I won't let him go to school anymore. He needs to go into a field where he might succeed by virtue of his pleasant personality'. This is typical of the schools at the time where children who were deemed to be unteachable were not worth bothering about by the tutors. With no system in place to provide people with learning difficulties and a set of standards that was expected of learners if a child was addle brained then they were dismissed from education.

Around that point in time slavery was the norm and people with no ability to learn had no opportunities. Instead they had to submit themselves to ownership of workhouses and wealthy households who would take pity on them.

 Fortunately, Thomas had a middle-class upbringing. His father Samuel was a political activist in exile from Canada and his mother was a school teacher and Nancy had a better way through the resources that she could provide him. The young Thomas was schooled from home reading books on science and philosophy and at one time he had an interest in the works of Shakespeare. He was a very avid reader and excelled in many of the sciences and mathematics. Later when his mother became stymied by his ever growing fascination another tutor came along to teach him how to handle advanced science and what it's practical applications could be used for. By the age of 12 he started to question the classical studies of science in electricity, mathematics, physics and engineering.

This home schooling story demonstrates how the possibilities of independent learning works for an autistic person. Thomas Edison can be considered as a poster boy for home schooling for people with autism. Autism is a neurological developmental disorder and that means that they learn in a different way. Rote and recitation is a bad method for autistics because it is stifling and it doesn't work well for people with mental issues. By making a person having to recite a rulebook you are rigorously testing and stressing their mental impairments to the point of breaking them. What Nancy Edison used to teach her son was a head and hands method in which Thomas had to learn through process and content, and empowered him to learn. She believed that not all valuable things in life were to be learned from books, it's okay to learn from life and work with your hands. My experience with school confirms this. I got more out of my life skills from self-teaching, distance learning and practicing science and engineering though my hobbies.

Although I support the integration of autistics into society as in accepting them for what they are I feel that some autistic people are worth tutoring to a system that works for them to excel in their own individual right. I support the selective schooling system rather than the one size fits all system used in comprehensives because it devalues the creativity and intellectual abilities of the individual. I do believe that it is right for the government to have selective education because it works for the types of worker they are likely to become. With autistics they each have their own interests and they should be allowed to study according the method of teaching that suites them. In the case of the fields they aspire to go into it allows their speciality to flourish. Especially if the school is autism friendly.

 Although there is an emphasis on people on the autistic spectrum in science and the arts there are also some whom are great orators and figures of authority who knew how to handle people. Some autistics do have great people skills and these are the ones who are likely to be verbal thinkers. One of the greatest leaders of a country who I have admired is the 16th president of the United States of America, Abraham Lincoln. Like me he is a right wing political leader who was among the first members of the Republican party. America's republicanism shares the same traits as conservatism, of which is also a philosophy that I endorse. Lincoln's presidency was mostly during the Civil War from 1860-65, which was fought over the question of human slavery. The Southern States under the Confederate government wanted to keep the slaves, but the Northern States of the Union wanted to disband all forms of slavery. There were a number of compromises that failed to settle the dispute and so the North and the South split into two different countries and then came the war.

In his road to power as the leader of the country Lincoln's life story was full of failures and defeats and facing overwhelming difficulties in life. Before he became president he had been defeated in eight different elections, had failed in two businesses and lost his fiancé to typhoid fever. Among other things he also had a history of mental health problems which in modern terms is classed as clinical depression. But he also had a number of symptoms which are attributed to autism. He was too trusting to his doctors, he suffered melancholy he was betrayed or unsupported by his allies in government and at one time he had suicidal tendencies and it is believed he wrote a poem about it in 1838 called 'The Suicide's Soliloquy'.

Lincoln kept himself in good health by delving into works of humour as a means of escapism from the difficulties of his ill health. One aspect of his personality that I find most appealing as an inspiration is his commitment to completion and fulfilling his life's goals. He was offended to the horrors of human dignity and the treatment of slaves and sought to abolish the practice of slavery across the whole of the United States. At that time Britain had already abolished it's own slave practices. Especially as he and many others believed it was against the republican principles of the Founding Fathers and stifled the progress of the nation and contradicted the principles of equality in the Declaration of Independence. Lincoln had set in motion the 13th Amendment to the Constitution to abolish slavery in America which was passed by Congress in 31st January 1865 by a vote of 119-56 and 8 abstentions.

Aspergers has a quality to it that makes people committed to a cause that will undoubtedly resolve a struggle that most other people would give up on. Lincoln had a purpose to commit to with his determination to end slavery and as a committed perfectionist he refused to give into the defeat of his impairment, his mental health or career problems. In a way I have had so many set-backs in life very similar to him and yet for some reason I still refuse to give into defeat. For me the right way is to make a stand no matter what holds you back. Your impairment might obstruct you but you have a purpose to fulfil and that struggle can only be hampered by a lack of positivity in your life. Although we have that mischief demon in our heard telling us we have no purpose to play with that madness and fight back against your demons. That demon is not a prophet, it's an awareness of our mistakes where action needs to be taken to better ourselves.

Reading was one of Lincoln's passions and he liked to regale people with stories about what he had read about to inspire his followers. He loved poetry and plays and with this he was able to become a great writer. Telling stories was Lincoln's way of making a point about his principles and policies. He combined logic and reason and he was a very intelligent politician, he would become generally interested in people and their problems. Ambitious, but a humble and extraordinary man with one of the strongest political achievements in the history of America. This is very much in keeping with the good qualities of an Aspergers person.

One thing that I have found out about the slave trade in reading about Lincoln is a footnote in the pages of history of how disabled people were affected by the slave trade. I have already discussed how disabled people can feel enslaved to their impairment's limitations. Although history tells us that blacks made up the majority of slaves these stories come largely from anti-racist campaigners and social justice warriors. Around that point in time there were also a minority of different slaves as well, of which these included disabled people. Despite the 13th Amendment emancipation there were still some slavery long after the smoke of the Civil War had disappeared. Of the four million slaves freed out of the Civil War around three thousand of them were classed as disabled. The slaves that were free had an ability to mobilise themselves into freedom because they were able-bodied. The disabled slaves however hadn't been able to gain that freedom in the same way.

 Now when I talk of disabled slaves I am not talking black people with impairments, but white people as well. The masters of these slaves were able to keep them long after the new laws were enacted because they felt that as disabled people had no means of working independently in a normal labour force. For that reason the owners could be entrusted to care for them in workhouses and asylums. Some of these disabled slaves eventually became free of their masters but were left to wander in freed displacement which meant that they had to admit themselves to asylums for the disabled. Since they couldn't physically help with the reconstruction of the country after the war they had no option other than to put themselves in a state of isolation from the mainstream. Working in these workhouses was a cruel and unforgiving practice which involved the disabled being put to work in menial tasks. According to the architects of the institution they could then go into the ordinary labour force with these skills, that's if any employer would take them on.

This is a practice that carried on well into the latter half of the 20th century until the disability discrimination laws were put into place.

Abraham Lincoln's conservative values are another example of an aspergic person being on the right and conservative. These values are recognised as the best qualities of an ASD person who can bring something great to the world. What values do people suppose that I could bring to the world as a right wing autistic person with conservative ideas or values?

I am among many other people with ASD understand the foundations of life that we need to start up the society and the country that we have to live in. We think in a one tracked minded manner known as monotropic, compared to multi-channelled thinking in non-autistics called polytropic. Autistics when properly matured are strictly disciplined in routine and laying the down the law through a process known as attention tunnelling. This is where we focus our monotropic attention towards a specific task or piece of information and our focus is kept straightforward in one direction. This is vital for providing us with the maps for life navigation.

Now in this attention tunnel our single subject focus on the foundations is very useful for things like policies, buildings, financial security, transport, telecommunications, etc. That's just for the basics of life that we need in order to grow food, travel across the country, have a nice decent place that we can live with all the comforts of home. This kind of thinking is found in many self-help books for ASD to manage their lives.

Some people may think that this is a limitation that maybe a weakness in a person with ASD. But if you look it in a positive way then you can see the greatness in it. That is to accept those limitations and use them in a constructive way for the cornerstone of civilisation.

People with ASD treat the footings of people's lives with the most care and attention as we need it to be. When you consider the material of the foundations and the soil it's set in you have to watch out for cracks that occur when the buildings above become too heavy and weaken the foundations. My observation and duty of care is due to my heightened interest in the matter than makes me highly motivated and work well. Although my attention is weak when divided between different subject matters in laying the foundation I can assign the right people to manage the different aspects of groundwork. I can give one person with a monotropic mind set a job of handling something within the groundwork like the management of the transport network or the running of the health service. Autistics are capable of visual thinking and when it comes to specific types of operations or information that are linked to areas of an autistic's interest, they can easily attend to them. This is because the information is locked into their attention tunnel and they can use their imagination to improve the efficiency and running of that part of the country. But that does of course include responding to feedback from the people within and using that public service.

Some people may use the way the media often portrays autism for the impairments it gives people to generalise them as unworkable for a career or even making a better world for that matter. It's like as if they don't agree with Hans Asperger but if you think of it that way then you are treating them as a broken appliance. That's not right. In fact it's far too simplistic – classing a disability more about looking at an un-ability in some situations. Even able bodied people feel disabled in certain situations which are unfamiliar and unrehearsed.

The best way to see an autistic to be able to prove a point is to recognise a disability in terms of being differently abled. That is to recognise the person's skillset as carrying out a task in an extraordinary way. We call this diffability. It makes life a lot easier to handle so that we don't have a negative effect on our self-esteem. Coming from this perspective we are more likely to accept good building material in our foundations. The material for this is the mental wellbeing and positive energy that we exhibit in our abilities, behaviour and choices.

Another of my best qualities is my geekiness, which is a quality that many ASD people have in their natural habitat. Mine is the appreciation and desire for innovation in science, technology, private enterprise and social mobility development. I have been an avid science geek all my life and I have followed the progress conducted by scientists, doctors, engineers, politicians and business people who have made great progress in making the world a better place. I have aspirations to become a scientist and to use my knowledge to advance the world as an inventor, an explorer, a researcher or a member of the establishment. Most people with ASD are renowned for their geekiness and use their knowledge and their special abilities in ways that could benefit society. As the autistic brain is capable of magnificent mental capacity for knowledge and wisdom so too can they teach the world better than an able-bodied politician who is incapable of researching for his own policies. Author Mark Henderson argues in his book 'The Geek Manifesto' that many politicians are unable to tell real science from pseudoscience and that it is impossible to create sensible policies about serious scientific issues for things like climate change, medicine, food production in agriculture and the running of developments in technology and infrastructure.

In my duties as an ambassador for the Science Museum in London I have shared my knowledge of scientific achievements in creative ways. I have had the honour of servicing Professor Stephen Hawking at the opening of an exhibition celebrating the work of British science in particle physics. Although I am not specialised in this area of science I have been able to tell visitors about the wonders of the universe right down to the small things that yield fantastic results. My favourite items in the museum were born out of crazy ideas from geniuses where some of them were on the autistic spectrum. I have a creation that contains an interesting story that puts the stereotypical portrayals of Essex to shame. Essex is often portrayed in the media as a county populated with lame brained, fashionable young people who live in towns with shops and bars with opulent working class lifestyle. Well I can tell you a story about Essex as a county populated with clever creative entrepreneurs who brought many scientific achievements that have revolutionised mankind's understanding of nature. Including developments in technology that make life fashionable as well as functional and invented many ideas that shape the world we live in. No one has ever heard of these county geniuses in popular culture.

One thing about science in society is that it's value is based on that it teaches us to be curious and inquisitive in nature. Politicians cannot ignore it. But what I find repulsive is the way they use it for policy based evidence, which is to use science to prove the usefulness of a policy that they find experts who can agree with papers they present to government. That is something that someone with ASD can verify and I can tell you from my own expertise that the way politicians use green issues and climate change policies isn't all that sound. There are a majority of scientists who disagree with global warming but they are living in fear for the sake of being demonised by green lobbyists who treat them as holocaust deniers. Al Gore, one of the champions of climate change awareness has a strong agenda with green issues that he has a watch list of scientists who disagree with man-made global warming.

When the green movement began in the 1970s it was about a campaign to promote issues regarding man's use of natural resources where they would become exhausted and we wouldn't be able to progress the world any further. But now that the governments of the world are actively tackling climate change there are some bureaucrats in power who are using this science to justify policies that are not properly researched. To them scientists are just tools for their policy making strategies. It is often said that if you put a scientist under political pressure then he'll do anything you like. In a recent flooding in Britain a government report was based on false evidence that dredging rivers to keep the flow of floodwater going doesn't work. Dredging does work because it spaces the width and depth of a river so that the water doesn't burst the banks. Something that you could easily learn in a primary school science lesson.

Autistics can really come into their own in politics by geeking up the UK Parliament or the US Congress. However there are few geeks in frontline politics because there aren't many examples serving successfully in office. But given that many geeks are on the autistic spectrum that lack of those in power can be remedied by the way they have the best brains. They can serve any political philosophy whether that be socialism, conservatism, liberalism, nationalism or communism. Their expertise is largely dismissed because they have little time or an ability to socialise actively to get the contacts needed for access to the corridors of power. For all the aspie geeks going into politics and business there ought to be more opportunities for those in the arts and sciences. In the west in places like Westminster and Washington science is regarded as a gaffe rather than intellectual honesty. It isn't any better for the artistic ASD side where their abilities are seen as a publication relations machine rather than a celebration of culture and national pride. They should see examples of how science and art with autism can be useful and ambitious using the examples of countries that excel in these abilities in the Far East.

In the last Parliament from 2010-15 there was only one scientist out of the 650 MPs. Most of them have backgrounds in journalism, politics and law with most of them in business. In the countries of the Far East like India and China they have members of government who have backgrounds in engineering and research. China's current president Xi Jinping studied chemical engineering, India's president Pranab Mukherjee is a major in political science, South Korean president Park Geun-Hye is a graduate in electronic engineering and Malaysia's prime minister Najib Razak has a degree in industrial economics. All leaders like these understand the need for cherishing the strength of their country's greatest scientific and artistic minds to develop their country's culture and national identity through economic development and investment in their brightest visionaries in their fields.

Since emerging into the spotlight a number of years ago geeks are now becoming more dominate than ever in politics and it has often been claimed that they will 'inherit the Earth'. I think that's possible and in fact it is happening right now especially as we are dependent on them in a world where I as an autistic geek am not expected to be normal, but show off and stand out and give the world a new way of thinking. Celebrated American physicist Richard Feynman declared that science is 'what we have learnt how to keep from fooling ourselves'. Geeks on the spectrum take this philosophy wisely. But there are few politicians that have an appreciation of geniuses. Not in an anti-science or anti-art way, it's just that they are indifferent or simply uninterested. That means they lack an understanding of the value of their gift when they should be looking to them for inspiration to build a better world.

CHAPTER SIXTEEN

Outside the concourse of Whitechapel hospital was building up with constant activity. There were more ambulances outside the station to bring the wounded in for treatment. The scene was full of countless sirens and flashing flights not only from the fire engines, police cars and from the man power of the emergency services calling out to their positions.

Scott's mobile ran, on the display was MUM and the clock readout was 15:00. For a long time he had forgotten all about June. He felt worried about her security even though they don't see each other eye to eye. He pressed the button to get his troubles out of the way. 'Yes hello, what is it?'

Where are you?' June's voice was calmly controlled as she heard her son's dismal reaction. 'I just saw you earlier on the news.'

'Oh good!' Said Scott. 'What do you make of my defence of mental health issues? I hope you didn't get the wrong impression that I was defending the bomber's actions, because I wasn't.'

'I wasn't thinking that.' Said June. 'I think you handled it well. But what I am concerned about is your welfare. You were on that train that got bombed.' panicked June. 'Only after I saw you on screen I thought, Oh thank God he's alive and well. I was worried sick.'

'Well as much as your concerned with my welfare I don't really care about it.' Said Scott. 'I'm not one to care about the feelings of loss. I can't even process those kinds of emotions.'

June was silence for a minute and then responded casually. 'Is there anything you want me to do? Where are you now?'

'I'm still at the hospital, being with my friends who I met today. What do you think?'

'What friends are these?' Asked June.

'These are people who I met on the train today in the wreckage. I helped them out.'

'What you were a first aider as well?' said June. 'You don't know first aid and what were you doing on that train. I thought you would have been at the Transport Museum.'

Scott's temper suddenly got rebellious. 'Well I think if you used your common sense you'd find that I was caught up in it. The journey from Auntie Jackie's place to the LTM went via the Piccadilly Line, I had to get off at King's Cross to get there and that's how I ended up on the train.'

'I'm sorry for you Scott.' June had forgotten the old basics of dealing with an autistic son. She had spent the night reading her old reference books on autistic spectrum disorders. When she saw where she had gone wrong, she accepted Scott's imagination to flourish for the best. Providing she could only say it to him in person, rather than on the phone. 'Listen I'm sorry about yesterday and, erm... well I just wanted to tell you that I had a bad night. I had been doing some reading on autism from those guidebooks I had on the shelf. I think we can work something out together. Maybe we could learn how to make our relationship better. This time I think we can work something out.'

'Well okay then.' said Scott. Although he felt slightly sympathetic he could project it in his tone. 'If you are willing to take an interest in mental health then I think we can improve our relationship.'

'That's good, I want to make a fresh start as well.' Said June. 'When will you be able to come home? Is it okay to come to the hospital?'

'No, it's okay besides I am taking the stories of my friends.' Said Scott. 'Something needs to be done and that is something that I need to take responsibility for. If I don't then I am going to have to live with the reputation of mental health being tarnished for the rest of eternity.'

June wasn't sure about what to make of it but she saw that her son needed to prove something positive. 'What does that involve?'

'That lawyer who I talked about on TV' Said Scott. 'The one who victimised the man that led to him blowing himself up. She's here with me and I gave her a right good hiding. I broke her ribs in the process and I showed her what mental health is capable of, defying the way they make us look like stupid sheep who need a selfish pig to speak up for them.'

'What?' asked June. 'You'd better explain that in person to me. Let's talk about that later.'

'Okay then, I'll catch up later.' Said Scott. 'I am going to have to go now and see how my friends are. Goodbye.' Scott hang up and went back inside.

The ward was bustling with activity in a manner of 'business as usual'. The ward has calmed down now and the patients from the train bombing has now come under control. There was some deaths just declared as Scott saw a list of patients declared dead as he past a receptionists desk. *These casualties could have been avoided if mental health issues were taken seriously. But how do people take seriously the kind of tragedy that comes with mental health. They struggle to find solutions because they don't bother to communicate with the mental health people themselves. They just go via practitioners and health experts leading to confusion and discontent.*

Back at the beds of his friends he found them talking about something that mattered to his nemesis.

'This is something that you might want to see.' Said Paul. 'Jane Glouster came looking for you. Apparently you telling people about her wicked ways don't matter to her.

'Why would she not bother?' asked Scott. 'Surely a powerful woman like her would have a reputation to defend, even if she has the attitude of a revolting goblin.'

'Well as it turns out at time of her last case where she won for the chemical company she had been planning on breaking up her law firm.' Explained Sarah. 'I don't know why, but it looks like she had been planning on taking early retirement.'

'Unless of course she has taken something out of her firm for herself.' Said Nick. 'I wonder if she has ripped off someone and made a closure to stop an investigation.'

'More likely she's got a pension fund stashed away somewhere for protection and she's running away from someone else whose out to defrock her.' Said Paul. 'My guess is she's making her next move.'

'So what can we do about her?' Said Nick.

'I think I had better find her and I think I know where she is likely to be hiding.' Said Scott. 'When I was coming to this hospital for my mental health issues all those years ago I used to go wandering off exploring the hospital.'

'So you know some good places she must be in.' said Sarah. 'Where is she likely to be hiding?'

'That's for me to find out.' Said Scott. He walked away and started to go on a search of Jane's whereabouts.

CHAPTER SEVENTEEN

Scott checked his watch; the time was 16:30. It felt like the day was so long it would never end. How could he pass the time so much in a short space of time and think the sun hasn't even come down yet? He got caught up in an accident, helped some people survive their ordeal, stand up for himself and for mental health, got hospitalized, talk to the media, found a story to write and made new friends. *How can one make so much progress in a short space of time and forget it even existed? Is time really an illusion?* More importantly he had to ask himself: where is the wicked vile woman who denounced him as a vulnerable, defeated and unintelligent being who was deranged to the point of sickness. It was her evilness that needed to be undone, she was in the wrong.

'Come on Glouster you revolting gargoyle, where are you?' he asked. Scott was walking through the places of the hospital he wasn't normally allowed into. It was like retracing old parts of his memory with which there was nostalgia. The times he spent in his youth attending these mental health sessions at the hospital allowed him to explore the parts of the hospital that off limits to patients. These days such action would be forbidden on the grounds of security fears. Eventually he found himself downstairs in the basement which has plenty of storage facilities.

Scott could hear some rather loud ranting coming from the other side of a wall where there was an open door. A woman's voice that no doubt sounded like the vitriol of a troll ranting about failure. If this were heard in an upmarket bar it would make no discerning difference whatsoever. As unintelligence goes the sound of a scatty lambasting witch it was. *So that's where she's hiding, but what could she be plotting?*

Turning the corner Scott listened out for the sound of the ranting. 'What the fuck.' She said. 'Is that all you've got? I've seen better service from a council estate skank serving me a fried chicken in a shop.' Said Jane viperously. 'There's a bloody good bill for infringement that will land on your lap, pikey.'

'You have a talent for spouting snobbish dribble.' said Scott. As she turned to see him she put a pack of cigarettes in her pocket, it looked like she was going to light up. To her right she had some big cylinders with 'Nitrous Oxide' written on them. It would be unwise to light up a cigarette so close to a gas canister even if the contents of it were non-flammable.

'Oh so you found me, great at last we can meet for one final time.' Said Jane, as if she was feeling victorious in defeat. Scott doubted her victory if anything was to go by. What could she have that made her act like a right show off. Her vile, shameless dastardly personality couldn't go far enough, could it?

'What's brought up down here then?' asked Scott. 'Hiding from the press, making a break for it to escape persecution. You really have a nerve.'

'What would you know?' said Jane.

'My friends told me that you were looking for me.' Said Scott. 'You said that it doesn't matter even though I may have ruined your business because you were breaking it up only last week after you glorified your clients and drove that man to suicide.'

'That's right young man.' Said Jane. 'I don't need it anymore. About a few months ago I started to lose money after I was caught having it off with one of my employee's husbands. But doesn't matter, he was only there for when I needed him to let off steam.'

'You mean you had been having an affair with your colleague's husband.' Said Scott. 'My God you really are a revolting gargoyle and probably a deadly scary witch for that matter. And also a profiteer and a vile hateful liberal fascist who believes in a right to spout pile at anything that disagrees with her even though your profession is about standing up for justice. I suppose you only got into the law profession to fight for the agenda of rich, powerful corrupt individuals like dictators and business people so that you can profit to fund a lavish lifestyle. How can someone for the likes of you stand up for human rights when you use them against humans.'

'We all make moral judgements.' Said Jane. 'It's just that people deserve more rights than others. You know having a right to property can be a much stronger case than getting justice for a victim of a car crash or in Craine's case a train wreck in human form.'

'By that logic we should reinstate the slave trade because slaves are property, not people.' Said Scott. 'In which case the employers who prefer foreign cheap labour to native workers wouldn't have to pay a wage at all to their workers. I haven't a problem with immigrants though, I can see the logic in why people refuse jobs that the immigrants take. It's because of the system that you fabricated to make them incapable of living an honest life. What sounds contradicting is that you live a dishonest life.'

'Oh please and you don't even have much experience in standing up for yourself.' Said Jane. Scott started to get filled with rage but this time he was determined to see to it that Jane would not take advantage of him yet again. He didn't need to punch her, he needed to upstage her. 'Besides have you in your career ever seen a story about a corruption case ever been written about. The majority of news stories don't even cover the scandals that most people have never heard of.'

'It's just because of the stuff that sells the papers that's all.' Said Scott. 'A celebrity gossip or an MP caught misbehaving is more likely to generate revenue than a case like what you'd expect to find out of a tyrant whipping his people into submission. Also the access to the story is another factor. When two cities have bomb attacks like London and Beirut a media outpouring is more likely to get better coverage and sympathy for London because a freedom of information is better here than it is in a foreign country with control over the media.'

'Oh really, well now I can understand why some of my clients don't like a freedom of information.' Said Jane. 'To them you are a parasite.'

'Well they are just as condescending as you.' Said Scott. 'People don't like being told what to think. Thought control is evil and they are only fighting to silence the press for the own agenda even if they are supporting a fascist dictator. That's not just hypocrisy when they speak up for poverty and injustice, it's a weapon to use against their opponents. Something that I have seen from North Korean propaganda material.'

'What, you listen to communist's propaganda.' Said Jane. 'That's a leftist doctrine.'

'I am not a leftist.' Said Scott. 'I listen to it for reference. Liberty is about the freedom to be wrong, not to do wrong. So by listening to all forms of criticism and compliments we don't embrace our progress in democracy blindly. One North Korean film that I saw explained how you as a lawyer for human rights abuses the system to enslave people to your way of thinking by stupefying them with excess pleasures.'

'It looks like you haven't tasted the fruits of liberty.' Said Jane. 'What would you do to make a better world when you are just a lame brained selfish twat. It's better that you stay safe and not show off because it makes you look stupid. That's why mental health people should be refrained from advancing themselves.'

'As a mental health person you think that I should be entitle to generous handouts and spoiled for fun.' Said Scott. 'Well that is just making me look like a slave to your agenda. Well I don't suffer the spoils of liberty or the fools who milk them gladly.'

'Oh God, another breadbasket who is hard to please.' Said Jane slyly. 'What could I do to fill your brain that could you see sense. You need looking after and you are totally deranged, the way you attacked me makes me want to put you in a zipbag and hang you out to dry. I'm sorry if the welfare handouts were not enough to convince you that you didn't need a job. It must be really embarrassing for you.'

'The only embarrassing problem I have is being made to feel like an inferior being by people like you.' Said Scott. 'Although I am not capable of empathy as an autistic person I can understand the problems that people have with establishment supporters like you. They feel like slaves to your politically correct feel good nature and doctrine. Speaking as a person who has had to put up with the stigma and useless services commanded by you I too feel like a slave but I refuse to accept your dogmatic vanity ideas that put me in a position of weakness. If you think I am just a reason for promoting complacent compassion, then you are wrong.'

'Complacent?'

'You are using disablement and mental health as a way to make yourself satisfied in a smug and uncritical manner.' Explained Scott. 'That's the trouble with charitable causes. They have no accountability to the people they provide for. Some of their achievements are masked and they use themselves as a money machine.'

'Yes of course they are.' Said Jane. 'I had a friend who ran a charity ball just to get up close with some soap stars. The ball might have raised some money but for what those poor bloody kids were worth we had enough to get pissed the day after on a boat cruise down the Thames. That's where it all started with my fella who hadn't had any action in bed for months.'

'Oh yes of course, I forgot that you're a homewrecker as well.' Said Scott. 'You slept with a man, break up your law firm so that you can put his wife out of a job, I suppose you've got a pension stashed away to save yourself as well.'

'Spot on.' Said Jane with glee. 'Much as I would like to discuss that with a humourless retard, I think you have a tendency to explode with rage like Mr Craine did quite literally.'

'Do I look like I'm carrying a bomb?' said Scott. 'Mental health people are not freaks or psychos that can be a danger to other people. You don't control them to stop them thinking violent and destructive thoughts, you're supposed to nurture their best abilities so that they can bring a shining light to the world that can make a peaceful and harmonious world.'

'They are too slow and stupid to learn.' Said Jane. 'They'd be better off caged, culled or sent to be outside the mainstream. That will teach them to be breadbaskets. As long as they can behave then we can live safely in the comfort of our own little world. You should be grateful for that, what's so awful about it? At least that way you don't have people pointing and laughing at you for being such a weird bastard.'

'So you are in favour of segregation as well.' Said Scott. 'The very thing that divides us. How funny is it that you talk of loving diversity but you don't want to see a lower class mentally ill person as a neighbour or a friend?'

'I support diversity on the terms that I can choose who I can live with just like you do.' Said Jane. 'It's just that I choose rich wealthy friends in Chelsea but not pathetic skanks or foreigners. As long as I can promote diversity and give those ethnic minorities want I want they want to have then I won't have to bother about them. And that goes for mental health as well, perhaps you'd like a five-star suite at Broadmoor.'

'So that's how you keep people in line.' Said Scott. 'Make people be thankful for their wealth and get them to shut up that way. It's such a travesty of modern liberalism. Thank God for conservatism, I think it's vital to protect liberty rather than the liberalisation to do something wrong.'

'That way of life grants you peanuts.' Said Jane.

'No Jane.' Said Scott. He reached into his pockets and pulled out a bag of peanuts already opened. Placing some in his hand he said, 'This is what peanuts are, they are a metaphorical object of what you, a rich spoilt brat with all the cosy associations of pigs have, that handout to people expecting mental health to use to live off and achieve nothing. Well from a former recipient of aid money and charity handouts from the rich, I can tell you they do me no good! So...' Scott threw the handful at Jane. 'You have them back right in your face you stinking champagne socialist skunk!' Then he took the packet out on her. 'And the packet as well.'

'It's ashamed you haven't got a tin because that would have dented my head!'

Scott angrily walked away and left Jane be. She turned to the canister and let open the valve. 'This will make a good laugh.' She said to herself. She understood that it was laughing gas and she felt it was needed to cheer her up. Jane then lit up a cigarette with her lighter. Without taking any direction she didn't realise her mistake.

In the hallway Scott could hear the lighter click lit and smelt a burning sensation in his nostrils. He realised that Jane had lit a naked flame next to a canister of nitrous oxide. *Nitrous oxide is also known as laughing gas, it's non-flammable unless you use it as an oxidiser for rocket fuel.* 'Oh God, she hasn't.' Scott didn't react very quick in a situation but realised that Jane made a fatal combination of nitrous oxide and a butane fuelled lighter with a piezo-electric spark. THEN.

Scott felt another explosion but this time he was not in the room. The store room were Jane erupted with a loud bang. Smoke followed quickly but there wasn't much that could envelop him. Clearly there wasn't much in that canister but just enough to make a small explosion that blasted the doors off their hinges. Scott walked back to the room where he could see that Jane was now dead, lying on the floor where she had been blasted against the wall. 'Just as I thought.'

The alarms in the hospital went off and an evacuation announcement took place. Although there wasn't a fire. Suddenly a security guard came down to see what had happened.

'What in God's name happened here?' he said.

'She had her last cigarette and it made her go out with a bang.'

Reflections: The Stigma and Neglecting of Mental Health in Society

The original novella was 'A Baffling Unoriginal Looking with a Voice to Prove Positive', which told the story of an autistic man who wanted to better himself in life. The second edition now known as 'A Puzzle in a Tunnel' tells the same story but in a different way and it still shows how brilliant people are being ostracised by mainstream society as unworkable. A man with bright ideas being segregated into a place he didn't want to be. One day he gets his chance in a train disaster where he helps some people to safety and in the process he comes across a crooked lawyer with a grudge against mental health. She had driven a man to suicide and took the lives of several dozen other innocent people to their deaths as a desperate cry for help. I made the case of Frank Craine's miscarriage of justice and the side-lining of him due to his mental health as an example to show that shows what happens when mental health is ignored. Then made to suffer as if that is what their life is supposed to be. This is the catalyst that makes Scott go to prove himself and speak up for the autistic spectrum community.

In the first edition Scott persuades Jane to commit suicide in a psychological rage and that is original for a crime thriller but not good for a case for challenging people's perspectives of autism in a good light. But for that edition I had to prove a point about the neglect of mental health. It wasn't going to be helpful if my protagonist was going to be vengeful with a psychotic rage. When I made these changes I realised that I had expressed my anger and worries in a grudge fuelled act of hate, and that was at a time when I was mostly introverted. That frame of mind was due to an inappropriate set of rules on equality that can unleash unimaginable horrors like self-destruction, suicide and mental breakdowns.

Like the invisible Ian Dury hit 'Spasticus Autisticus' I have a novella that is also about a refusal to accept enslavement to the limitations brought about by a disability. It doesn't end on a good note but it does go to show that blood can be spilt when injustice has not been settled in an effective way. There are problems in this world that result in death by political correctness and neglecting the needs of special people. Needs which are only ever used by politicians and social justice campaigners who see me with my impairment as a force to use for their own personal and sometimes selfish interests. Like pigs who take advantage of the weak as they boast of their intelligence claiming to be the prophets of liberty.

When I first released this novella I had a feeling that some people wouldn't understand what kind of message I was trying to put across. Maybe I didn't express myself properly as the story is written in a directed perspective from my point of view through Scott Hardy. But that's how you are likely to see a fiction novel written by someone on the autistic spectrum. I never got any proper social skills training so I didn't know how to handle a two-way conversation or relate to another person that well. This social awkwardness can be seen in the way that the novella has been written.

One reviewer said of my novella that it had a style similar to Irish novelist James Joyce. Whom as it happens is also believed to be on the autistic spectrum. One book in particular that was made in the comparison was his best-known work 'Ulysses'. I have read this novel and explored it's content and structure and found that the two of us do have a likeness in our style. Ulysses has an unconventional structure with an alternating non-consistent format of storytelling where it moves from first person to third person and reporting mode to play script style. It toys with the reader's imagination as it explores the social demographic of life in Dublin in 1904. There is a report on his style examined by Irish psychiatrist Paul J. Whelan. In it he explains that Joyce had a technique known as 'stream of consciousness'. A technique that is akin to thought disorder. If that is what explains his bizarre style in his writing, then it looks like Joyce's way with words describes numerous emotions elaborated by various thoughts and processes. Joyce's style and mine is a result of poetic beauty and creative manipulation of language. Hence the elongated vocabulary in both our books, so that doesn't make me an exception.

For this last chapter I am going to conclude with a message of hope and opportunism for the benefit of the autism community. I originally gave Scott an ending which demonstrates a negative aspect of being autistic as a semi-deranged psycho who hides his wrong doing. But here there is a change of setting and the demise of Jane Glouster. Instead of being killed by Scott in a deranged psychosis, she is undone by her own carelessness.

As I have already revealed in the previous chapters I have been told that my right-wing views and ideas that disagree with charitable causes for autism have been a negative aspect of being disabled. That murder suicide scene is just one example of how bad a mentally ill person can become when society fails them, or in some cases an injustice that results in making a parasite out of someone with a mental health impairment. I do have prejudiced and ablest thoughts and there plenty of people with other disabilities that think so as well. This negative attitude comes from the way we are lost and forgotten about in society and it is a dangerous thing to think so. If you allow mental health to go unattended then you will leave those people affected to walk into a minefield at risk of doing something wrong. I'm not saying that we should control the thoughts of people with autism but teach them how to understand people and then it won't be so insufferable. Such inaction can lead to a disabled person feeling isolated, hate filled and full of contempt for others that they wish their neurotypical counterparts dead.

It has often been reported that people with mental health conditions are the kind who are most likely to commit murder in some horrible way. Statistical studies have disproven this over the last 20 years. One of them was made on the crime rate in Sweden in connection with mental health disorders in 2006. As it happens only 1 in 20 people with severe mental health problems are likely to commit violent crimes. Only 18% of murders and attempted murders are committed by people with a mental illness. Mentally ill people with prejudiced thoughts are not likely to commit murder and I am certainly not one to be capable of killing people. I don't have grudges and am not judgemental about a person's actions in a way that makes me angry enough to be vengeful.

But there are troubles with the healthcare services available that need to be addressed. When I had my bad moments with my mental issues I had to wait months to get a meeting with a psychiatrist just to get cognitive behavioural therapy. Such therapies like this should be readily available on demand. They are relatively cheap and easy to provide than hospital treatment for physical injuries. In June 2012 an academic report stated that mental issues are very much under-treated on the NHS. Mental illnesses can increase the scale of physical illnesses and that if psychological therapies are readily available then the outcome will mean that the cost of physical injuries will drop dramatically.

The difficulties in getting the right treatment stokes tension in the community and it leads to a stigma just to have a mental health impairment. When I was diagnosed with autism it was like being given a death sentence that you were going to be hung out to dry if you shared your vulnerability with the world. I feared that if I lived out my life being labelled with a mental health condition then I would be ostracised and made to accept that I was weak and defeated. Despite my rights to certain liberties I was not given any opportunities to achieve my full potential. Einstein said that 'Everybody is a genius, but if you judge a fish by it's ability to climb a tree then it will live out it's whole life believing that it is stupid'. I can easily relate to a fish like that and so can many other autistics. The way I was brought up by a judgemental society run by an elite of patronising pathetic social justice warriors was like by ordered about by an overweight Napoleonic pig rearing other people's children to think that they should entrust their care and attention to a false parent.

George Orwell's novella 'Animal Farm' is a book recommended for conservatives and freedom lovers that teaches us of the temptations to freedom that become slavery using animals in the place of humans. Orwell himself isn't a conservative but some of his books are recommended for conservative thinkers as they have themes to back up the claim that socialism doesn't work. Especially for people on the autistic spectrum. In Animal Farm there is a revolution led by pigs that went wrong as they pervert the course of their fight for freedom and bring the other animals under their control. The pigs are led by a Stalin like character called Napoleon who provides reading classes for the other animals. As it turns out most of the animals are illiterate and that constitutes an impairment which makes them vulnerable and for Napoleon to take advantage of. Disabled people including those on the autistic spectrum have impairments such as this. The way Napoleon controls his citizens like this is similar to that of what I went through when I was deemed unfit for purpose and refrained from advancing myself by my school and appointed care workers.

According to Napoleon in Animal Farm the pigs are the brainworkers as they are the smartest and most capable readers on the farm that they deserve to be the natural leaders. But that logic also implies that the other animals are inferior in a manner similar to disablement. The pig's selfishness and the other animal's lack of knowledge creates a superiority complex that conceals a sense of failure so that the animals feel superior under the guidance of Napoleon. The way the pigs dictate that their superiority is in their knowledge reminds me of those good for nothing campaigners that preach for compassion but deliver no solutions for me to achieve my potential. They didn't see much potential in my kind which are dismissed as they see us as weak, ridiculous and full of energy but without strength on our own.

This lack of trust and patronising attitude to disablement offends me to the core. The way I see it the welfare system acts as a mechanism to make mental health feel no need to try. The authorities and social justice fighters think we are bound to their leadership as if we should not try to be independent. This is also seen in Animal Farm where one pig called Squealer explains to the animals that Napoleon believes that' all animals are equal but some animals are more equal than others'. In other words some people deserve to be treated equally but although that is true some people deserve better privileges because of their power, strength and influence. Napoleon believes that the other animals, in which we can think of them as the mental health, are likely to make the wrong decisions in life and that they are likely to commit a terrible indictment that will stain their character. This is the socialist way of crushing criticism and rebellion. I am a rebel amongst those with a mental health condition but I have committed no such crimes against society or humanity other than to free myself from the constraints of those who put a barrier up against my goals.

People on the autistic spectrum may be loyal and committed to their friends and the basic order of society but not to the point of bowing heads down to a master of no principles who disproves of independent thought. 'Napoleon is always right!' said Squealer to the other animals. Well as all creatures were created unequal in life so must all forms of thinking so no one person is ever always right. We should be mindful of the kind of care and attention we receive in life. Some people use their compassion and arguments as a manoeuvre to get rid of their opponents and those whom they consider to be a bad influence or have criticism that can defeat them. I have had some people use my disability against me in the past and it is not only discriminating but hateful and tactically vile. Political activists and social justice campaigners are not always on good terms with those whose battles they fight for their cause.

Do you know how the people who orchestrated the system that cared for me can relate to those Orwellian pigs? Their judgement of my abilities was like that of a saying that Albert Einstein had about genius. Einstein once said that 'Everybody is a genius, but if you judge a fish by it's ability to climb a tree it will live it's whole life believing that it is stupid.' There are many people who can relate to a fish by a modern education system that only makes fish climb trees, but makes them climb back down and make a ten-mile run. I have seen pigs in human form push me about with my anti-progressive ideas and institutionalised inspired policies on the welfare of mental health and other forms of disablement. I hold them to account for trying to undermine mental health instead of nurturing it. I don't need to be lectured by an overbearing patronising social justice warrior who expects me to think alike him. Any doctor will confirm that no two brains are the same.

There was a time that affected me about mental health that really offended me so much that I had to take action. During the European Union Referendum, just a week before the vote the Member of Parliament for Batley and Spen, Jo Cox was murdered by a lone deranged gunman called Tommy Mair. I was a Leave campaigner supporting and promoting the case for leaving the EU in a positive way to promote British economic growth and opportunities for better ways of doing things beyond the confines of the so called European Superstate. In the hours after the killing Mair was arrested and charged with Cox's murder. I remember thinking at the time that the campaign was starting to get ugly and the two sides were starting to spill blood, as if a riot was soon to be on the scene. Only a day before Cox was amongst a flotilla of boats with upper class establishment figures and wealthy celebrities and business people on the River Thames in London. They were making obscene gestures and vulgar remarks to fishing industry workers who were promoting the case for leaving the EU as the regulations from Brussels had devastated their livelihoods. The attitude of some of those counter protestors was like watching wealthy elitist snobs sneering and shooting at poor peasants for fun.

This is no way that I would conduct my campaign in justifying a vote to leave the EU. I often say to fellow activists 'fight your enemies with honour, not scumbag yobbery'. What is the point of fighting for a better world if we act like animals to get what we want? But Jo Cox's murder wasn't anything from Leave.EU using aggression and wickedness, it was from a man with a mental health problem and in some way his local council had not provided well enough for him. Tommy Mair had hoarded fascist material many years before the referendum. This is not a fanatical Leave supporter but a seriously disturbed person who I can understand from a perspective of a person with mental issues of his own. When you are made to suffer the effects of your mental illness with no form of healthcare or specialist treatment you end up with a time bomb waiting to go off. Mair is just one example of a failed society that let down a mentally unstable person who asked for help. We have stressed about this before and when we see it happen some people care only for the effect of the incident rather than the problem itself. That is a way of making capital out of a crisis for political, financial and personal gain.

The murder of this sweet innocent woman was turned into a political manoeuvre by the Remain side. I remember in the fall out of the killing there was some disturbance amongst the mourning. Some Remain activists accused Leave of secretly recruiting far right fanatics to attack their opponents. Proclaiming that the people that I was campaigning with were dangerous and unhinged. One Remain campaign director Will Straw told Stronger In to actively use Cox's death on the grounds that Leave were using 'division and resentment' in the UK. Of all those things they said I am not mentally unstable however much my Aspergers affects me. My ability to campaign is not in a negative way. I think they were doing disablement whose rights they had fought for a disservice and making me with my disability as a radicalised psychopath. That attitude made me realise that they saw no good in me for bettering myself but just to use me as a puppet for their political propaganda. Besides throughout the referendum both sides were using fearful tactics to persuade people to vote their way. This was known as 'Project Fear'. I however was using a peaceful and constructive message in my campaign without having to be hateful. Only a morally bankrupt disgusting carcass of a person would use foul and sadistic language to justify their position.

I really feel sorry for Jo Cox, her life was about caring and showing compassion for those most vulnerable. She really doesn't deserve to be a martyr and I think Remain should hang their heads in shame. Although I am not very good with empathy there is something about this that affects me on a personal note. The Remain camp took advantage of the death of a mother and a political case out of it as the attacker was a mentally ill perpetrator. He had been abandoned by the lack of care from his community and this is an example of a society that fails in the duty of mental health. I am not sympathising with Mair or defending his actions I am trying to make a point about a duty of care and respect for people on the autistic spectrum.

One of the things that I highlighted about this was how the most vulnerable have been abandoned and left to fend for themselves. I often wonder if the leftists can see how their inaction has consequences on human life. Mental health are unable to achieve their true potential because they are unable to care for themselves and that makes them lonely and paranoid. I was sickened by the way some of the left and Remain used this murder and Mair's psychosis to further a cause. Well they have only given me more than a good reason to resent them. Why should I as an autistic person accept the welfare support of a group of people who use me as a pawn for their game against the right and the conservatives to further their fight for civil rights. I am not interested in their misery; I am interested in positive thinking.

On the weekend of what was supposed to be a day of suspended campaigning out of respect for Jo Cox I went canvassing for Leave. Remain and Leave had agreed to suspend campaigning that weekend but some Leave and Remain activists continued to canvass and gave excuses for their actions. This however was a low key campaigning day for both groups. But Remain groups still took advantage of Cox's death for political advantage. Labour councillor Anne Lee from Kettering District Council wrote on Facebook that they had "to do all we can to avert the Brexit disaster" and that the Leave camp stood for the "cold blooded murder of Jo Cox". I felt that was so horrible and immoral to go to lengths to promote a vote for Remain that I had to take action. But what made me feel so related to it was that they were taking advantage of a mentally unstable man's impairment. All could think was: "Is this how much they value my sense of purpose as a disabled person? My mental instability making me a psychological weapon to be let loose and set upon the party's opponents. My only usefulness to their benefit is a radicalised psychopath to kill other people so that they can gain political personal gain?"

I am not a puppet of a master or a devilish cretin to be set upon some poor innocent person. I may not know empathy but I am not a deranged murderer. I seek justice not through vengeance but through looking for mutual cooperation for a better way. I may be socially awkward but I am not stupid or frightful, I am a rebel with a cause. What you can't do though is ignore me. If some patronising pathetic do gooder thinks he knows better, he will grant me an opportunity and test my abilities and my power. I was brought up in politically correct society that looked down on me and led me to believe that I cannot be trusted to decide my own destiny. It was like being controlled by an Orwellian-Stalinist inspired pig operating under a doctrine that I am a pet and use me to protect their own selfish interests. Well in the years that I matured I realised that I was stronger than they are and their teachings were wrong. To compartmentalise a person like that is to shunt them into a state of oppression. I will not be patronized and made to feel a slave anymore and I will not be used as a puppet for political propaganda for a leftist agenda or even a pet for a socialist bigwig.

From the autistic spectrum to the master of normal land: 'You failed to keep me bound, I am a free man with an imagination to run wild and make the world a better place. I do not want your pathetic peanuts for my care, I want an opportunity to be someone with real money to fill my heart's content. You try to attach and pull the strings upon my soul, I'll cut them and bound you with them. Then as you watch me with all my might and power I will show you a better world.'

References

http://siteresources.worldbank.org/DISABILITY/Resources/Regions/South%20Asia/JICA_Bangladesh.pdf

https://www.theguardian.com/society/2016/feb/13/mental-health-services-crisis-britain-revealed-leaked-report

http://www.communitycare.co.uk/2013/11/20/chronic-underfunding-mental-health-care-stigma-proving-hard-reverse/

http://www.disabilityplanet.co.uk/critical-analysis.html

http://dsq-sds.org/article/view/112/112

Atlas Shrugged; Rand, Ayn (1957)

The Fountainhead; Rand, Ayn (1943)

Animal Farm; Orwell, George (1945)

Nineteen Eighty-four; Orwell, George (1949)

Brave New World; Huxley, Aldous (1932)

Brave New World Revisited; Huxley, Aldous (1959)

United Politics: 'Autism on the Right and Conservative'; Keeble, Charlie (2016)

A Baffling Unoriginal Looking with a Voice to Prove Positive; Keeble, Charlie (2007)

The Geek Manifesto; Henderson, Mark (2013)

www.ingramcontent.com/pod-product-compliance
Lightning Source LLC
Chambersburg PA
CBHW071210240726
48654CB00009B/724